Lessons Learned on Bull Run Road

Shellie Rushing Tomlinson

Lessons Learned On Bull Run Road

Shellie Rushing Tomlinson

Lessons Learned on Bull Run Road

Acknowledgements

To Cyndie and Rhonda, my big sisters and fellow members of the
Bull Run Road gang: Thanks for the memories.
To Mama and Papa: Thanks for loving us enough to teach us right
from wrong. I think most of the lessons stuck!

To Melbourne Community: Thank you for a special childhood.
To my best friends, Rhonda and Debbie: Thanks for your support
and feedback. You must've gotten so tired of hearing these stories.
To Betty Stone, Doris Sullivan, Connie Schneider, Debbie
Fortenberry (and anyone else who helped me with this project that
I pray I'm not overlooking): Thank you for your time. If there are
still errors in here, I'll tell everyone they're mine.

To my husband, Phil: You are the best. Thank you for loving me
and encouraging me to see this through.
To my children, Jessica and Phillip: I hope I've taught you at least
some of the lessons my parents taught me. I love you.
To Christ my Lord: May something in these words testify to Your
love; that is my greatest hope.

Introduction

Lessons Learned on Bull Run Road shares the values three little girls, my sisters and I, learned while growing up along the Mississippi River. In the last few years, many stories of the Louisiana Delta have found their way into the major newspapers. They've all told sad tales of economic woe and racial tension in an area of the country the media has called the poorest place in America. I know that Delta, but it's not mine. In *Lessons Learned on Bull Run Road,* I hope you'll find the Delta that I love.

Everyone today is talking about the redefining of America's families. *Lessons Learned on Bull Run Road* will take you to a place where family is defined amidst a tapestry of work and play. It's true—not everyone grew up in a happy family. These readers are invited to let the Bull Run Road gang, along with their parents, cousins, grandparents and friends fill the empty holes in their hearts—if only for a time. For everyone else who had a normal childhood, in a normal family, in an average town, I would hope that after reading this book they'd discover that normal is quite wonderful after all. Time is a thief that often steals our past. If the stories told here could bring smiles of recollection, if they could sharpen faded memories and recapture feelings long forgotten, my vision for *Lessons Learned on Bull Run Road* will be realized.

TABLE OF CONTENTS

LESSON NUMBER ONE
"Play Now or Pay Later"

Mama taught us to appreciate people's differences...

Poor Mama, she exhausted herself trying to smooth the rough edges of her little girls. Mama was a true "Southern lady", a natural beauty born the second of five to a Baptist preacher in Natchez, Mississippi. Her innate grace helped make her a basketball star; her black hair and bright wide smile topped a tall slender frame and earned her the hometown title of "Miss Forestry Queen."

Mama's marriage to her high school sweetheart ended shortly after she brought me, her third daughter, home from the hospital. Biological Dad was more interested in cards and liquor than diapers and bottles. Mama was raising three little girls on a clerk's salary, when a young man she'd known as a child came to town and dropped by to pay her family a visit. It'd been years since he and Mama had seen one another. By this time Future Papa was fresh out of the service and farming a plot of land in Alsatia, Louisiana. For the next year or more he made the two-hour trip to court Mama. My sisters and I were their ever-present chaperones. I was two, Rhonda was three and Cyndie was five. We rode in the back seat of Future Papa's car and sang along with Mama to Conway Twitty's new hit song, "Mississippi Woman, Louisiana Man."

It wasn't long before Papa married us, taking his prize bride and her tiny wedding party to the Delta to live on Bull Run Road. He built her a little white brick home with 900 square feet. She kept his castle spotless and worked beside him in the fields.

Mama looked as much a lady driving Papa's bean truck and grain cart during the day, as she did on the piano bench at Melbourne Baptist Church—twice on Sunday and once on Wednesday night. Manners were important to Mama; a theme most of her lectures centered on, as she constantly schooled us

Lessons Learned on Bull Run Road

in the things little ladies did and did not do. Unfortunately for Mama, my sisters and I had a hard time differentiating between the two.

Mama should've had at least one little girl who was proper—someone who liked to dress up and play tea party. Instead, she got Cyndie, Rhonda, and Shellie, (that's me there on the end), three tomboys. Rhonda might've came the closest, everyone did call her Pretty Woman, but being the middle child and painfully shy, she didn't stand a chance—Cyndie and I took her down with us. Most of our capers were birthed in Cyndie's fertile mind, with me badgering Rhonda into being our unwilling accomplice.

When Mama wasn't cleaning house, cooking a big meal, or helping Papa in the field, she liked to have a lady friend over for coffee. Life on Bull Run Road was pretty isolated with only one other house for miles, and our cousin Jimmy Ray lived there. But, we'll get back to Jimmy later.

Our job was to play with the visiting lady's children. Most of the time we only had each other to play with, so Mama thought it should be a real treat to have new friends. My sisters and I thought our club was complete; and for the most part we considered these intruders weenies, babies, girly-girls.

One summer day an old friend of Mama's came to visit. Cyndie, and Rhonda and I eyed her daughter warily as she emerged from the car. Our assessment paused at her feet. One of our major criteria was the absence or presence of shoes. Unless it was the dead of winter we went barefoot, and we were suspicious of those that didn't. Our circle had a hierarchy, and those with the toughest soles were accorded the most respect. We smiled sweetly until the grownups went indoors and then we hit Visiting Girly-Girl with a little Bull Run Road initiation.

If she'd walk the side rails of the bridge by our house, we'd consider playing with her—an honorable test in our estimation. This bridge was probably ten to fifteen feet high, and walking its rails never gave us a moment's pause. Many of our days were spent there. In the spring, if the drainage ditch below was full of water, the rail might be our tight rope and we the daring circus performers. During the summer months, when the bed was dry and cracked and strewn with the fragile, pinkish-white skeletons of crawdads that had escaped my sisters and me in the spring, it turned into our fort. We slid beneath the rails, and perched on the sloping sides of the ditch, hiding from the marauding Indians. Cyndie could describe those vicious red natives with their sharp knives and penchant for blond hair in such detail that Rhonda, the only fair head in our fort, would cry to go home and I'd end up with nightmares.

Stoically, my sisters and I led our potential playmate to the site of her evaluation. Upon our arrival Cyndie instructed me to assume my position on the bridge's rail and demonstrate the initiation requirement. Poor Mama! Just as we expected, our guest refused and went tattling to her mother, like the baby we knew she was. Visitor Lady, and her crying girly-girl on one side of the table, and we three lined up like wooden soldiers on the other. We felt totally justified, but you couldn't miss the message in Mama's eyes: "Play now or pay later."

Mama excused herself and took us to the back room. She explained that there were many different kinds of people in the world and we better find a way to get along with the ones that weren't just like us. She said there was something you could learn from everyone you met and something about most of them that you could enjoy, if you gave him or her the chance. Then she glanced towards Papa's belt on the dresser and smiled encouragingly. We decided then and there to give Visiting Girly-Girl another chance.

All the ways of a man are clean in his own eyes, but the Lord weighs the motives. Proverbs 16:2

LESSON NUMBER TWO
"Pride goes Before the Fall"

Mama always told us that pride goes before the fall. One day we saw it for ourselves...

We grew up on Bull Run Road in a cluster of farming families called Melbourne Community, right in the heart of the Louisiana Delta. Our corner of the world was merely a bump on Highway 65 between Tallulah and Lake Providence. Except for the family that owned the local grocery and the preacher's family at the Baptist church, almost everyone we knew lived off of the land. And from an early age my sisters and I recognized that our livelihood revolved around its whims.

Each year the first hint of spring signaled the beginning of the cotton season, and the community began to buzz with activity as farmers prepared their land and equipment for planting. At the same time, in stubborn opposition to the farmers' plans, the spring rains would begin, bringing with them the familiar threat of flooding.

Parallel to Highway 65 ran a long, high, snake-like mound of dirt, a man-made levee system that struggled each spring to keep the mighty Mississippi River from overflowing its banks, and swallowing us whole. It was there along the levee that the Corp. of Engineers staged a continual battle with Old Man River, working around the clock to bring in tons of dirt and thousands of sandbags. While they struggled to strengthen the levee's walls, the churning river chiseled relentlessly at her sides from within, forcing our community to live with the constant danger of a levee break.

For weeks the adults would talk of nothing else, until one day the rain would stop abruptly—as if someone had turned off a huge water faucet, and the farmers would breathe temporary sighs of relief. Only a couple of short months later when summer settled in and one hundred-degree days baked their thirsty young crops, these same men would hold their hats in one hand, and scratch their heads with the other, as they searched the skies and prayed for rain.

During these early months of the growing season, while the crops were maturing and the days were growing longer, my sisters and I embraced the large blocks of free time given to us each afternoon after school. Our farm was a giant adventure land we never grew tired of exploring. We were an early version of latch key kids: if the weather were pretty Mama locked the latch and we played outside. She had a lot of cooking and cleaning to do, and we "weren't going to be underfoot."

Together we invented a game called "chase-don't-touch-the-ground." And, like everything else we did on Bull Run Road, it wasn't a game for the faint-hearted. Papa's tractor shed was the playing field. Here we jumped from tractor to combine, swung from rafter to rafter, slid down poles, and crawled over the two-story roof. All to avoid the chaser, who was jumping from tractor to combine, swinging from rafter to rafter, sliding down poles, and crawling across the roof to get to be the chasee. In spite of the rules, we hit the ground more often than I care to remember.

Another of our inventions was just as much fun and twice as likely to end badly. This time Papa's shed was a great racetrack, carved out around the heavy farm equipment. The players rode bicycles, and there was only one way for the chaser to get to be the chasee—knock someone down. It wasn't enough to run into the other girl's bike; she had to crash. As the youngest, I was always "it" first. This meant I was subject to Cyndie's ever changing rules:

"I said twice, Shellie. You have to get someone twice before they're it."

As tough as we thought we were, we couldn't hold a candle to the Shumates and Goulettes, two families with kids that made *us* look like girly-girls. Rocky Shumate and the other boys would challenge us to a game of dare. They said, "climbing tractor sheds was for babies." To prove their point, these geniuses would take their bicycles on the roof, and ride them off! My sisters and

Lessons Learned on Bull Run Road

I never managed this feat. We wanted to, and we meant to. But at the last second, we always ended up throwing the bike one way and jumping the other.

Not all of our activities were this dangerous. Crawdad fishing was one of our less painful pastimes. Crawdads lived in the shallow water of drainage ditches that ran beneath the wooden bridges dotting the roads of Melbourne Community. The fishing was easy; a ball of twine confiscated from Papa's tractor shed, a kitchen knife, (Mama's scissors worked better, but taking 'em was too costly), and the fishing was on. We'd cut a length of string and tie a piece of bacon on the end. Crawdads loved bacon! You could watch their little pinchers close around it if the water weren't muddy from too much rain. And if it were muddy, you just waited for the nudge the old crawdad would give you. The trick was in the timing, jerking the string up and over your head so the crawdad would smack the road and lay stunned long enough for you to avoid his pinchers and pick him up.

Crawdads are aggressive little creatures. We liked to watch them rear back on their tails and wave their pinchers around wildly. They looked, to us, like miniature versions of the animated dinosaurs we saw on Saturday morning cartoons. Another distinguishing characteristic of the crawdads is their strong odor. They smell *bad*—like the worst fish you've ever smelled, times two. Even the black gumbo mud beneath the bridge took on their odor. (I don't know why people called the black land "gumbo mud," unless it's because it's thick and tends to ball up around the plows and planters.) Most evenings Mama sprayed us down with the water hose before allowing us inside for a real bath.

One day my sisters and I were crawdad fishing a little piece from the house when a neighbor girl came cruising up on her new bike. Little did we know Mama's lesson on the consequences of pride was about to play out right before our eyes.

Cyndie, Rhonda and I tried to hide our envy with indifference, while Neighbor Girl pedaled back and forth on the bridge. Her new wheels had the latest braking system: instead of the brakes being on the pedals, they were on the handlebars. And if you hit the foot pedals to stop, like we were all accustomed to, you weren't stopping and you were likely to skin your bare toe on the road when your foot slipped off.

18

Shellie Rushing Tomlinson

On her last fly by, Neighbor Girl must have intended to skid up to the rail and stop to see how the fishing was going, or maybe she had planned to taunt us one more time... We'll never know because she forgot about the new brakes, and hit her foot pedals instead. She went into a free fall—bike and all—right over the rail and into the water. It wasn't a long fall, and the water couldn't have been more than a couple of feet deep. Who could blame us for hooting and hollering all the way home? Let me tell you who...Mama!

Pride goes before destruction and a haughty spirit before a fall. Proverbs 16:18

LESSON NUMBER THREE
"That's Your Real Daddy... and Other Important Information"

I learned on Bull Run Road that a daddy isn't always a blood relative...

Though I was pretty young the first time I heard of Virginia's letter to the newspaper editor—the one where she asks if there is really a Santa Claus—still, I knew immediately the girl didn't have a big sister. I was convinced of this because Rhonda and I got most of our information from Cyndie. I'm not suggesting this was a good thing, all I'm saying is Cyndie would've spelled the Santa Claus issue out for Virginia much sooner, and a whole lot clearer. I was only six when I learned the hard truth.

The object of my obsession that particular Christmas was a soft-bodied doll with enormous blue eyes and wavy blond hair, a dream doll that cried "mama" when you turned her upside down. (I don't remember anyone questioning this design feature at the time.) I didn't just want that doll, I *needed* that doll—and I made sure everyone knew it! Cyndie must've grown tired of hearing it. One day she took me by the arm and covertly dragged me to Mama's closet, where she promptly climbed onto a chair and produced my heart's desire from the top shelf.

"Now, see there! I told you they were getting you this stupid doll. And I'll promise you another thing, too. If you tell Mama I showed you, I'll beat you up for sure."

My dream baby was waiting for me under the tree Christmas morning, and she was even more beautiful than I'd remembered. I noticed Cyndie pausing from her own treasures to give me a warning glare. Experience had taught me she'd make good on her threats, so I got busy singing Santa's praises to Mama.

Shellie Rushing Tomlinson

Some of Cyndie's secrets were more powerful than others were. It was several years later when she spilled the Big One.

Mama was our family beautician and every Saturday night Cyndie, Rhonda and I lined up single file to have our long locks washed and rolled. Mama shampooed our hair in the kitchen sink, and Papa combed us out before putting us back into her assembly line for the pink sponge rollers. We begged them to change jobs—Papa's big hands weren't very gentle with a comb. Mama also cut our hair, and as we grew up we tested her talents with our requests for the latest hairdos.

The day the big secret was spilled, Mama was trimming Cyndie's hair in the kitchen. Cyndie was twelve, practically a teenager, and she was coveting a "shag", the fashionable look of the day. Mama's competent scissors were flying fast.

I'd been rummaging around in the attic during Cyndie's appointment. Mama was almost through with my sister's new look, when I walked into the kitchen carrying a picture of a strange man. For several years Mama had been trying to find the right time to tell Rhonda and me something important. To Cyndie, there was no time like the present. Totally unaware of the bomb in my hand, I asked in all innocence,

"Who is this man?"

Mama froze, but Cyndie didn't; she looked up and said sarcastically, "That's your daddy, dummy."

"Yeah, right. Papa's out at the shed."

"Not him," my big sister said coolly. "He's not our real daddy."

Mama recovered after a minute or two, and began to breathe again. She rounded up Rhonda and Papa, and we went into an immediate family council meeting with a focus on history. Neither Rhonda nor I had any memory of life before Papa, but Cyndie had been old enough when Biological Dad left us to remember him. Knowing her as I do, I still can't believe they kept her quiet that long.

Although in Papa's heart we were already his girls, he'd wanted to adopt us officially for years. Cyndie's announcement just served to put the wheels in motion. That summer a lady from the state came. She took Cyndie and Rhonda

21

Lessons Learned on Bull Run Road

and me into our living room, one at a time, and asked us questions. When my turn came she asked me if I wanted Papa to be my daddy. Seeing as how Papa was already my daddy, I thought she was either being silly, or it was a trick question. I wondered if Cyndie and Rhonda had got it right. I finally answered yes, but that wasn't enough for her. She wanted to know *why* I wanted Papa to be my daddy. The only thing I knew to say was that I liked him. Fortunately, that seemed to be the right answer.

A few months later Mama dressed us all up in our Sunday best for a trip to the courthouse. And once everyone there signed a ton of papers, we became Rushings in the eyes of the law. After the proceedings my sisters and I were led into a side room and I met the man whose blood runs in my veins. I watched him talk to Papa and Mama first, and then to each of my sisters, and then he stooped to hug me—I felt nothing. He was a stranger, but I was told to be nice, so I hugged him back and asked Papa if we could go home.

All things work together for good to them that love God, to them who are called according to His purpose. Romans 8:28

LESSON NUMBER FOUR
"Sisters in the Hood—Country Style"

I learned about accountability on Bull Run Road as Mama and Papa joined together to teach us the principle of sowing and reaping...

The Good Book says, "Spare the rod and spoil the child." As far as my sisters and I could figure, Papa and Mama weren't taking any chances. Their rod of choice was usually Papa's belt or a flyswatter. Although, if your crime occurred outside, like say at a church picnic, they liked to play "Bring me a switch." This was a favorite game among adults, but a lose-lose deal for us kids. We had to pick out a switch and bring it to The Switcher, who would proceed to strip it of its leaves. You could pick a good one, or risk making them madder if they had to go for a replacement. Since we weren't given a lot of time to spend on selection, and experience had taught us the smaller switches were the best at stinging bare legs, we usually played the odds and brought the biggest one we thought we could get away with.

Many of our offenses occurred at church, which wasn't at all surprising as often as we were there. One Sunday morning Papa and Cyndie were singing in the choir. With Mama at her customary position on the piano, Rhonda and I were left sitting alone. We were admonished to be on our best behavior; I'm sure our intentions were honorable.

Rhonda started it. I can't remember how, but I'm positive she started it. (Most people thought Rhonda was the sweet one with her innocent blue eyes. I knew better, I shared a room with the little brat.) The skirmish started small, a push here, and a pinch there. Papa eyed us from the choir loft. Rhonda declared us at war by taking my little black patent purse and dropping it on the shiny linoleum floor. Looking at me with an evil smile, she took her matching black patent shoe and kicked it under the pew in front of us. The conflict had escalated, and there was only one thing for me to do. I dropped Rhonda's little black purse and kicked it harder. My enemy and I both gasped with disbelief as

23

Lessons Learned on Bull Run Road

it slid all the way to the front...coming to rest at Mama's feet. We could feel Papa coming before we saw him.

Actually, if we were bound to get a spanking, we would've chosen Papa for the administration every time. He had a slightly impaired whipping style. Papa held the switch in one hand and the offender with the other. He would swing, and we would run in circles around him, jumping each time he swatted. If you got your timing just right you could actually avoid most of the licks, and the ones that did land would be pretty harmless. While we danced to Papa's beat, we hollered from our supposed pain, fully aware these pitiful cries would break his heart. When Papa couldn't stand it any longer, he'd hug us and say how he hated having to do that, but it was for our own good. We ended these sessions feeling sorry for Papa.

Mama had no such weakness when she set out to discipline, but then she had to spend a lot more time on it than Papa did. She required you to lie on her bed face down, where she'd begin to whip your bottom, promising that you wouldn't sit down for a week. Mama never lied. It was always tempting to cover your compromised backside with your hands to try to shorten the experience, while beggin' for mercy and promising to never commit the offense in question again. This move was a bad idea. Mama would just get those fingers until you got them out of the way. Mama would be through when Mama got through! She had her own post-switching line, too. Mama expected us to believe these sessions hurt her more than they hurt us. Sure, we might've been country kids...but we weren't stupid.

Our oldest sister, Cyndie, had this whole "sisters-in-the-hood-country-style" thing going on back then. It was us against them, parents vs. kids. She had her own rules, too, and she was serious about the first one: never let 'em see you cry. Cyndie thought it gave them too much satisfaction. Rhonda and I would be caught in that well-known spot between the rock and the hard place. We would want to cry because maybe Mama would stop early; but Cyndie would be there glaring at us, daring us not to. If you cried too easily, or too loudly, you had to face Cyndie later. At times like that, it sure was hard to be at peace with both Mama and Cyndie.

"Whatsoever a man soweth, that shall he also reap." Galatians 6:7

LESSON NUMBER FIVE
"Story Telling, a Family Tradition"

My grandmother taught me to value and to learn from the experiences of the aged...

I guess I get my story telling honestly. When I was growing up everyone told stories, long ones and short ones, funny ones and somber ones. Sundays in Melbourne Community were some of the best story days. In the mornings we listened while the preacher told well-rehearsed stories from the Bible. And after services we either went to someone's house to eat and visit or had company over to our house. The food was always fantastic. But I liked the visiting because that's when the best stories were told.

We had a family friend named Pop Searcy who could tell some really good scary stories. Nobody did a better job with bloody bones and black-eyed peas. If you've never heard this one, your life experience is incomplete. Remind me to tell it to you sometime.

The best storyteller of them all had to be my grandmother on Papa's side, Ola Mae Rushing. She lived alone several miles away from us in a small house with green shingles. My Grandmaw Rushing was a hard working, sturdy woman from the hills of Kentucky. She met and married my Grandpaw when she was eighteen. After moving around a lot during the first half of their married life, they eventually came to Melbourne in a 1937 dodge pickup and settled into farming. Grandmaw used to tell me how they had started off keeping house in a tent. She told me how she'd made a broom out of sticks and used it religiously to keep the ground swept as clean and hard as the linoleum in her wood frame house.

My Grandmother and I were very close; I guess because I always knew I was her favorite. I knew she thought I was the smartest and the most talented and I bloomed under her approval. Grandmaw hadn't had a lot of education and

26

she was proud of my infatuation with words. When I was nine years old she bought me a typewriter for Christmas and I pecked out a novel on it called *Martha and her Horse*. Grandmaw loved it. I wish every child could know how it feels to have an adult that thinks whatever you say is worth hearing and has the time to listen while you say it.

Grandmaw and I entertained each other. Sometimes older people find it hard to get people's attention. But, I enjoyed hearing my grandmother reminisce. And did she ever have a lot to say! She'd birthed ten children of her own and raised them to adulthood, along with an extra one that wasn't hers, but needed to be.

My Papa was next to the youngest. There wasn't any other adult at home when Grandmaw went into labor with her last child so she anchored the tail of Papa's baby dress under the heavy bed in her bedroom. This was the closest thing she had to a playpen and she reserved it's use for emergencies; even then she'd put a dab of honey on the little one's fingers and give them a feather to keep them busy. After Grandmaw finished giving birth she cut the umbilical cord and checked on Papa. This story was fascinating to me. From what I'd seen so far, women that had babies went to the hospital for days and came home looking weak and tired.

As a young woman Grandmaw Rushing took her children to the field to help Grandpaw handpick his cotton. The ones that were too young to work would be left on the ends of the rows watching over the newest baby. Grandmaw and the older kids would tote their sacks down the rows until the bags got too full and demanded to be pulled. She'd tell them stories as they worked to keep their minds off the hot sun bearing down on their backs and the scratchy husks rubbing the skin of their fingertips until they produced angry blood blisters. And at regular intervals she'd stop and nurse the baby while the working kids quenched their thirst with a thermos of water she'd brought from home.

I never knew my Grandpaw Rushing. He died before we came to live on Bull Run Road. One summer day he came in from the field at noon and sat down on the sofa to rest. Grandmaw went to the kitchen to fix him a plate of her good cooking. When she called him to the table he didn't answer and he didn't

27

Lessons Learned on Bull Run Road

come. She found him dead on the couch from a massive heart attack. He was sixty-eight years old.

Her husband's death hit Grandmaw Rushing hard! By this time she had lived a very full and difficult life; all of their kids were grown and she was tired—so she quit. She just got through and quit. She spent the next thirty something years sitting in a green chair by a window in her living room. I heard the adults whispering about it; they wanted her to get up and out and live. Not me, I listened to her stories and I knew she was tired. Besides, I liked her there in her chair.

Grandmaw didn't mind being by herself during the day but she didn't like to stay alone at night. Sometimes I'd get off the bus in front of her house to spend the night with her. I always knew where I'd find her—in her chair.

The adults also talked about how heavy she was. As she got older her feet began to swell from the extra weight she was carrying and her ankles turned out in awkward directions, making it hard for her to walk. I knew everyone else thought she was too fat. But I liked her heavy—like a rock.

Grandmaw saved her best tales for bedtime, scary stories that made my mother angry and dissuaded Rhonda and Cyndie from staying the night with me at her house. "Why does she tell her that stuff at night?" Mama would ask Papa. "It gives the baby nightmares." And sometimes it did, but did you know there are times when it's fun to be scared if you're lying by your grandmother in the dark and you know you're really safe? It's a way to be face to face with everything bad you were ever afraid of and knowing at the same time that it can't really get you.

One of her stories went like this. She said that late at night ever since Grandpaw Rushing died she would often hear someone coming through the rusty front gate, and then into the house—and then walking through the house with a chain. She said she'd call out, "Claude, is that you?" and she knew it was even though he never answered. And then Grandmaw would say, "Listen, listen Shellie, do you hear that?" And we'd both hold our breath and listen while the hair on my arms stood straight up. All these years later it still does.

I was a married woman with two kids when my parents had to put Grandmaw in the nursing home. She hung on a lot longer than the doctors said

28

she would, proving to everyone how strong she was. My mama took great care of her. And when Grandmaw's mind failed Mama washed and wiped her face and bottom like Grandmaw had once done for so many others. I admired Mama. It was all I could do just to see Grandmaw like that. But I forced myself to come as often as possible. I'd watch my Grandmother and wonder who she'd been before her body got so tired from scrubbing floors and picking cotton. I tried (without much success) to picture her as a young Kentucky girl with big dreams.

Grandmaw was still telling stories from long ago a good while after she'd forgotten who we were or where she was. Only then she had reentered them; I thought this was fitting. In the end, her memories became her present and we became her past.

The beauty of the old men is the gray head. Proverbs 20:29

LESSON NUMBER SIX
"Ringlets, Hemlines and Black-Patent Shoes"

Mama said ladies were polite. Papa said Mama was one tough lady. By watching her, my sisters and I learned how to be both...

My sisters and I might not have always acted like the little ladies Mama groomed us to be, but when we stepped off the bus at Transylvania Elementary School, she made sure there wasn't a trace of our tomboy selves visible. Mama spent a lot of hours at her sewing machine making our wardrobes. As the baby of the family, I became very familiar with these outfits. I saw them first on Cyndie and then on Rhonda, before inheriting them for the grand finale.

Every school day, Mama dressed us in her ruffled creations, our long hair forming ringlets down our back from the dreaded pink rollers we'd spent the night in. On our feet we wore the standard black patents, polished to perfection with Mama's elbow grease, and a little Vaseline petroleum jelly. You can only imagine how popular these costumes were with us. But we didn't get a vote; Mama was serious about our grooming, as it was a direct reflection on her and Papa. We were 'gonna make them proud—or else.

One day, Rhonda's first grade teacher got a quick lesson in just how serious Mama was about our fashion. This teacher, we'll call her Miss Nameless, decided that particular day that Rhonda's dress was too short for her tastes. So, in front of the whole classroom, Miss Nameless laid Rhonda over her lap and took the hem out of her dress with blunt school scissors. Rhonda walked around the whole day with her frayed hem hanging below her knees. Being the shy one, she was much more embarrassed by the public display on the teacher's lap than by the sloppy statement her hem was making.

I don't remember any of us girls thinking the dress thing was a big deal. That afternoon we got off the school bus and Mama took in Rhonda's new look before firing off a couple of questions in a frighteningly quiet tone. Seconds later, we were loaded into the family's brown Dodge and heading back towards the school. I think Mama's face and the speed with which we were moving told us quickly that we were having a big deal after all.

Mama didn't scream and holler that afternoon, but she did have a lot to say. The principal and Miss Nameless didn't get to say much at all. Before we left, Miss Nameless took a needle and thread, kindly supplied by Mama, and put that hem right back where she found it. Mama might not have given her girls much slack—but woe to the outsider she suspected of mistreating us. One weekend her wrath was unleashed uptown...

Saturday was Mama's big shopping day. My sisters and I went with her to town to buy groceries at the A&P Supermarket. We'd jump around the store behind her cart, trying to stay on the scattered black tiles. Sometimes another shopper would get in the way and we would have to step on the hated white background. Mama should've been more patient with all this activity, we were doing it for her—"step on a crack, break your mama's back". Coincidentally, this is the earliest memory of my recurring flying dream. I would sail and drift around the top of that big old store while Mama demanded I come home that very minute. Cyndie and Rhonda always looked jealous in my dream.

Sometimes, if we promised to be good, we got to go to the five and ten next door and look around while Mama finished her grocery shopping. My first and last brush with the law came there at the TG&Y dimestore.

I skipped my six-year old self into the store and headed for the candy aisle, carrying my little black Sunday school purse with me, along with a few coins I'd managed to save. The candy aisle was overwhelming, causing me to spend a long time on my deliberations, looking in my purse several times to try and make my coins and my selections even out.

Finally, I made it to the front and placed my choices proudly on the counter, beaming at the saleslady. She stared down at me without returning my smile.

"What do you have in that purse?" she demanded coldly.

I didn't really understand her question, but her whole attitude scared me. I started to call for my sisters but before I could get another word out, she snatched my purse out of my hand, unsnapped it, and turned it upside down. Instead of the stolen goods she expected, my little coins rolled out and over the

31

Lessons Learned on Bull Run Road

counter and onto the floor. Tears gushed from my eyes as I bolted for the door, leaving my savings behind.

Mama was putting her groceries in the car. In between sobs and hiccups, I managed to tell my story. I was still jerking as I followed her back to the dimestore. She marched past the checkout counter and straight to the manager's office for a little heart to heart. I held onto Mama's hand and wiped my face on her dress while she laid things out for him. The manager called Miss Security in over the intercom. I remember both of them standing there while Miss Security apologized to me. I flinched as she reached to pat me on the back, a thin smile on her wrinkled lips. It was a long time before Mama traded with TG&Y again, and to this day, you can't pay me to open my purse in a store.

"Even a child is known by his doings, whether his work be pure and whether it be right." Proverbs 20: 11

LESSON NUMBER SEVEN
"Tornado Alley"

Papa and Mama showed us girls how to be a good neighbor...

By the summer of my eighth year I had begun to spend most of my time in a large Formosa tree in our front yard. Imagining myself as an undiscovered artist, I'd sit in my perch and try to draw and write wonderful things. But my greatest passion was reserved for reading and my hideaway was perfect for it. My seat was an old limb that had grown wide and smooth, its shape similar to Papa's comfortable recliner, while above my head a marvelous leafy green canopy shaded my haven and offered me the privacy I craved. I also had my own escalator, an exit plan as quick and efficient as the pole in any firehouse. My special limb grew right beside my perch and when I jumped out and grabbed it the whole thing would droop with my weight and deliver me within a foot of the ground. Life was good.

Growing up in Melbourne Community meant my part of the world was small and sheltered. But, I learned early that books could take me right past its borders and into the big, vast world beyond. Once a month the bookmobile from the East Carroll Parish Library came lumbering down the road. Cyndie and Rhonda could've cared less, but I still remember the smell of the books and feel the kiss of the air-conditioner on my skin when I opened the door. The morning it was scheduled to run, I'd be out in my tree right after breakfast. From the top of my perch I could see for miles. I'd have my stack of conquered books with me, and my mind would be racing with the possibilities to come, row upon row of words I'd never read.

On my first glimpse of the slow-moving library, I'd ride my leafy slide to the ground and loudly announce its arrival. I could never stir any excitement in my siblings. If they did come aboard, they rarely left with a book—and on the rare occasion they checked out one, they lost interest quickly. It didn't take long for me to realize that their loss was my gain. I was only allowed to check out a

Lessons Learned on Bull Run Road

certain number of books, a number I devoured long before the bus's return. If I could manage to get my sisters to check out their allotment of books, I could read those, too.

A couple of summers ago my teenage daughter, Jessica, worked at the East Carroll Parish Library. One day she got to go out on the bookmobile, an updated vehicle with many of the same books. That night at supper I asked her if she had waited on any little girls that jumped on early and stayed on too long. I asked her to be patient with the ones that couldn't decide which treasures to leave behind. And then I told her about another little girl keeping watch from the top of a Formosa tree many years before.

I was very protective of my leafy green home; no one was allowed there without an invitation. But as difficult as I found it to protect my home from unwanted guests—I was powerless to guard her from the forces of nature.

Each spring, when conditions became favorable, Mother Nature began to churn out whirling, angry beasts to ravage the South. If the weather watches came early enough, the community would begin to prepare. Having seen plenty of upturned trees from earlier storms, I'd watch my Formosa Home nervously from the front window of the living room.

Scientists have identified a phenomena know as "tornado alleys", familiar paths that see more than their fair share of tornado activity. For a time, Melbourne Community found herself sitting squarely in such a path. Right before a tornado strikes, the air gets really heavy and very still. It seems as if everything around you pulls in its breath and hangs on tight. There are rules to surviving a tornado—places in your home that are more safe than others, specific windows that should be opened to encourage the right flow of air. The National Weather System never suggests keeping a good sense of humor. With all due respect, I think they err by omission.

When the tornado warnings came, Papa would turn the living room couch upside down, making our own little padded shelter that we gathered beneath to pray and wait. Waiting was hard for us kids, often spurring my sisters and me to find ways of passing the time that Papa and Mama found less than amusing.

Cyndie would generally open the meeting. "I call to order this meeting of the Rushing Family Tornado Club." She'd recognize the members that were able to return and ask for the reading of the minutes from the last meeting, whereupon the current secretary would begin...

"We just met last week, same time, same place. I took minutes, but the paper got blown away."

One of us would make a motion to move to another state and we'd laugh, or someone would suggest we serve refreshments next time. We thought we were very witty, but Papa and Mama would scold us for being ungrateful. With theatric whispers we'd thank these guest speakers and break into fits of laughter. Sometimes, if we weren't too annoying—and the danger wasn't too ominous, we could see our parents smiling at each other in the glow of Papa's flashlight. I guess we all needed something to ease the tension.

It wasn't unusual for us to see sheds blow across open fields, and pieces of lumber wrap themselves around heavy equipment like the pliable sticks of a child's modeling clay. We knew the dread of hearing the roar of a killer tornado's approach, and we knew the relief of surviving when it was gone as quickly as it had appeared. But scariest of all were the tornadoes that came at night. Then we could only imagine the damage—and my imagination was vivid.

As soon as the storm was over, the phone would begin to ring and Mama or Papa would race to assure the caller that we were okay, asking anxiously about our neighbors in the same breath. Like many other families in the community, my parents were quick to take in our less fortunate neighbors. Mama would put on a pot of coffee for the arrival of these shocked survivors who showed up cold and wet and shaking from their losses. Mama offered them dry clothes and food and a place to lay their heads. I was always surprised at how different these adults looked when they arrived; they were always smaller than I remembered, and more fragile. One night the King family called for help. Their grandmother's house trailer had been demolished and she was missing. The men went to look for her while the women and children gathered to pray for God's help. She was later discovered wandering around in a field, disoriented but alive.

After surviving several of these harrowing experiences, Papa had an underground shelter installed in our yard. Our newest Family Convention Hall had a much larger seating capacity than the upturned couch. Papa even had one of these shelters put in at his mother's house down the road.

35

Lessons Learned on Bull Run Road

The monster tornadoes eventually changed their path and the adults relaxed; I was just as relieved that my Formosa hideaway had escaped destruction. My tree still stands in the front yard of our old home, though it has grown and matured over the years. I like to think that its strength testifies to the many solid friendships of Melbourne Community born and nurtured in the face of adversity.

Thou shalt love the Lord thy God with all thy heart, and with all thy soul, and with all thy mind...and thou shalt love thy neighbor as thyself. Matthew 22: 37-39

LESSON NUMBER EIGHT
"One with our Ancestors"

I learned on Bull Run Road that an idea that first offends your conscience will become more comfortable the longer you entertain it...

My sisters and I considered foraging for our food to be an important part of our heritage. My mother's father had a lot of Indian blood; his mother had been one-half Cherokee. Cyndie, Rhonda and I were proud of this heritage. We liked to think we were part native as well; sustaining ourselves on what we found in nature made us feel "one with our ancestors".

Through our early foraging expeditions we established four major food groups that the USDA has yet to recognize. First, there were sweet clover and honeysuckle. Both of these were in abundance right at our feet. But, as food sources we felt they were too predictable. So we graduated to sucking on salt tablets from the big bags Papa kept in the pump shed. Papa used these tablets to soften our hard country water. We used them to prove to each other how tough we were.

I hesitate to mention this next food group because plenty of you won't believe me. But it's true nonetheless. We scraped tar off of a big black gasoline tank and wadded it into balls. These we stuffed into the corners of our jaws and chewed them like the men did their tobacco. Combined with saliva, the juice from this tar made for good thick streams of black spit, and made us feel plenty tough. This roughneck attitude could've also been instrumental in the problems that developed with our neighbor one summer when we foraged a little too far from home.

Mr. Wall lived across from us on the Sand Road. He was the prototype of the avid gardener. If he'd ever worn anything other than faded overalls, we wouldn't have recognized him. Every spring we'd watch him plant and nurture his seeds from infancy until harvest, and months later his efforts would be rewarded a hundred-fold—just like the Bible says. Mr. Wall would gleam with

Lessons Learned on Bull Run Road

pride as rows of his sweet yellow field corn waved beside the fat green snap beans, bragging to anyone who'd listen that his plump red tomatoes would've bowed their host plants to the ground had they not been tied upright on wooden stakes.

As appealing as all of this produce was, none of it got our attention like the big juicy watermelons that grew on the far end. Mr. Wall monitored them carefully, turning each one every day to make sure none of their sides rotted from lying on the ground. His were some of the best melons a person could expect to find in the parish.

Although Mr. Wall was generous with this luscious bounty, each year we became convinced his melons were ripe a good while before he did. It was during one of these impasses that we decided to take matters (or watermelons) into our own hands.

It was a brutally hot delta summer day the first time our desire for Mr. Walls' melons got the best of us. We invaded his patch and made off with one of his big beauties. Back at our place, we broke it in pieces and ate as much of the evidence as we could, before hiding the remains in the tall grass along the ditch bank.

I was most miserable that evening at supper. My stomach rolled and tossed throughout the meal. Mama's concern for my lack of appetite only made me feel worse. All I could think of was *thou shalt not steal* and having broken "one of the big ones", I was convinced I was dying from eating the stolen goods.

When morning came I was surprised to be alive. But the conscience is a decidedly fickle thing, and after several days passed and nothing horrible happened, I began to accompany Cyndie and Rhonda back to our neighbor's watermelon patch for more of these afternoon raids.

It's been proven that if criminals continue to get away with their crimes they become overconfident and lazy, prone to making a mistake that eventually trips them up. This must've been what happened to us.

We had no idea Mr. Wall was on to his missing watermelons that fateful day as we set out to snatch another melon, entering his patch single file, oldest to youngest. Suddenly, Cyndie tripped over a string and set off a terrible racket.

My heart commenced beating loud enough in my chest for me to hear in my ears. We'd made a tactical error in underestimating our opponent.

Tricky Mr. Wall had strung together dozens of empty cans and laced this heavily laden string out of the patch, into his house and right up to his recliner where he sat with a firm grip on the other end. He was outside hollering at the top of his lungs before we knew what was happening. Mr. Wall had been certain the watermelon captives were some boys up the road—he was as surprised to see us as we were to see him.

Our captor marched us back to the house to face our parents' wrath. Stealing from our neighbors? The look on Papa's face was frightening. The fact that before long Mr. Wall would've given us as much as we could eat made our crime twice as bad in his eyes. Papa said we couldn't have been that hungry— and he was right; we weren't. We wanted to explain, but we sensed that Papa was in no mood to hear about the importance of foraging.

Once we apologized to Mr. Wall, we were left alone with Papa. He told us that we should be wary of any activity that we felt compelled to hide. And then he questioned us about how we felt the first time we stole one of Mr. Wall's watermelons. My stomach rolled at the memory. By the time he asked us how our feelings had changed over the past few weeks, he didn't have to explain any further. His lesson was clear and permanent.

For there is nothing covered that shall not be revealed; neither hid, that shall not be known. Luke 12:2

LESSON NUMBER NINE
"Hard Work and City Cousins"

Papa taught us that hard work was something to be proud of...

Mama might've missed having little ladies, but if Papa missed having a son, we never knew it. He took his three tomboys and put us to work on the farm. Papa liked to tell the other men there was nothing their boys could do that his girls couldn't do better.

Sometimes our city cousins came to visit. They'd stay with our grandmother. (These were strange kids—they'd *beg* to go to the fields with us.) Still, city cousins can provide a lot of fun. Their visits usually provided us with a different form of entertainment, along with another round of spankings. My sisters and I weighed the cost of "educating" them and considered it worth it.

One day we were out of school for spring break and working in the field with Papa. He was planting beans and we girls were filling the hoppers, lifting bean sacks that weighed as much as we did and replenishing Papa's planter when he came around empty. Accustomed to the weight of the sacks, one of us would stand in the bed of the big truck and throw a sack down to the fellow worker waiting below. It would give you a nice little jolt—but we could stand our ground.

Much to our displeasure, we were also entertaining; a certain city cousin was out on break, too. The night before he'd begged Papa to let him come to the field and help. City Cousin watched us briefly before deciding he could handle the bean sacks if we could. We knew he couldn't, but that didn't stop him from starting in.

"Hey, throw me wan." (Although he meant to say, "throw me one," I have deliberated misspelled it in an attempt to mimic his accent. None of 'em could talk right.)

"You can't catch it!"

"Yes, I can," he argued, "throw me wan."

"It's too heavy."

City Cousin stomped his foot. "No it's not! You guys throw me wan or I'll tell Aunt Charlotte and Uncle Ed."

Cyndie, Rhonda and I caught each other's eyes. City Cousin was standing right in front of a big drainage ditch whining about wanting to catch a heavy sack. There comes a time when you have to give someone what he asks for. We didn't feel responsible for City Cousin swimmin' with the crawdads, but Mama disagreed!

Our jobs changed with the seasons. Once school let out for summer and the crops were up and running, Papa paid us a dollar an hour to hoe cotton and beans. Mama would wake us and make breakfast while Papa sharpened the hoes for the day's chopping. Outside a truckload of laborers would be waiting; Papa was an equal opportunity employer a long time before it was politically correct. We were a multi-racial group bound by need; theirs to earn a dollar and Papa's to teach his girls the value of an honest day's work.

In the mornings the cotton would be wet with dew, and by late summer the plants were almost over our heads. This meant our clothes got soaked right off. Although no one liked getting drenched so early, we learned that everything was relative when the sun climbed high in the sky and beat down on us unmercifully.

Our job was to walk a row of cotton plants looking for offending grasses like Johnson grass or cuckleburrows. These hardy trespassers had to go. If the weeds were allowed to remain mixed in with the cotton, they lowered the price Papa could get for his crop. When we found the unwanted grass, we chopped it down with our hoe, being careful to avoid damaging the precious cotton plants. (Please, allow me a sidebar here. One time our neighbor's granddaughter, another city kid, set out bright and early one morning to "chop" cotton for her grandpa. Not real clear on the procedure, she had leveled the first two rows of mature cotton plants before her grandfather found her and took the hoe away. Is it any wonder that we didn't think much of these city kids?)

As the day wore on, the rows seemed to grow longer, and the water coolers waiting at the ends of the field seemed to get farther and farther away. This prompted us to invent imaginative ways to cover the ground. As novices we plodded along tending to one row each, but with experience we learned a really

Lessons Learned on Bull Run Road

good hand could walk in the center of one row, while monitoring the two neighboring rows at the same time. Papa was the final judge on who was a novice and who was not.

Sometimes things livened up quickly if you happened upon a snake. There are many poisonous and nonpoisonous snakes in Louisiana. The Cottonmouth, Rattlesnake and Water Moccasin are a few of the dangerous ones that shared our Delta. We were taught to recognize them from an early age. Here are a couple of life lessons: a snake is a poor opponent for a sharp hoe; and your foot is a poor opponent for a sharp hoe. One day Rhonda and I were racing the others to the end of the field when I swung at a big cuckleburrow weed and contacted the arch of my foot—I still have the scar to prove it.

Hoeing could be hard and dangerous work, but there were a few perks for us girls. If we were working close to the house, Papa would take us home early for lunch so we could watch our favorite show, "The Young and the Restless." Mama usually had a big meal ready; and if she didn't, she had thick slices of bologna from the country store. When I hear the word "bologna," (and we pronounced it "ba-lone-ee"), I don't think of the thin almost odorless slices you find in today's gleaming supermarket. I think of stiff white paper folded around chunky slices of pure heaven, each piece of meat encircled with its own red wrapper.

Of course, we felt obligated to complain about hoeing, but I'll never forget the pride I felt at payday. Papa would come home with a whole stack of one-dollar bills and count our wages out into our eager little palms, one dollar for every hour. We were rich, and Papa said we could do whatever we wanted with our windfall—just as soon as we set aside our tithes to the church.

Wealth gotten by fraud shall be diminished, but he that gathereth by labor shall increase. Proverbs 13:11

LESSON NUMBER TEN
"Open Frog Surgery"

Mama taught us that kindness begins with compassion for all God's creatures, great and small...

My sisters and I never intended to be heartless. Maybe it was because bumblebees were abundant in our Delta come spring; maybe that had something to do with us drafting them. Or maybe they just looked like fun with their chubby black bodies and yellow backs, like short squatty men with daffodil colored vests. One thing for sure, nothing about bumblebees suggests trouble like, say, a big red wasp does. A kid can take one look at a wasp and know it's angry without anyone telling him. For whatever reason, watching the bumblebees whizzing around the yard one day inspired us. I can't remember who suggested it first, but somehow we hit on the idea of flying them like kites.

Through trial and error we discovered that the ones with black noses would sting but the ones with the yellow noses wouldn't. A trip to Mama's sewing box produced thread and, at the expense of the first few participants, we learned exactly how tight we could tie the thread around their little bellies without accidentally dividing them in half. When you hold a bumblebee in between your fingers they hum furiously, producing an odd vibrating sensation that tickles your fingers. Sometimes this would give me the giggles and I'd have trouble holding on to them long enough for Cyndie and Rhonda to tie the thread. But once we got the tension right, we'd let out the thread and our buzzing friends would take off with us running hard and fast behind them. When Mama found out what we were doing, she said we were being cruel and we should be ashamed. I was surprised and sad. I had thought the bumblebees were having as much fun as we were.

43

Lessons Learned on Bull Run Road

Mama was no happier with the incident that prophesied of Cyndie's future medical career. My big sister Cyndie is a registered nurse today, but she was married with two kids before she went back to college. Cyndie had always wanted to be a nurse. At thirty-two she decided to pursue her dream. It came as no surprise to me; I knew my big sister was destined for the medical profession from the day I assisted her in her first open frog surgery.

Cyndie was probably eleven at the time, which put me around eight. She found a big toadfrog in the ditch out front and convinced me that he needed surgery. Always eager to please Cyndie, I ran and purchased medical supplies from Mama's sewing box and Papa's shaving kit. Cyndie's first step was to pin our wriggling patient to the picnic table—belly up and spread-eagled.

"Scapula," demanded the surgeon.

I placed Papa's single blade razor in her hand without flinching. Cyndie deftly opened up the little patient while I watched. (I don't know where Rhonda was, but I can guess she didn't want anything to do with our unwilling green participant. Cyndie and I had already made a habit of holding her down and making her choose between kissing our green friends or repeating whatever we wanted her to say. These coerced confessions usually involved pledging her love to some boy we all found revolting.

For an inexperienced surgeon, Cyndie was very methodical. She took her time and showed me all the parts of the miniature patient, including his still-beating heart. I guess you could say it was exploratory surgery by nature. When the procedure was over, Cyndie closed up with needle and thread before removing the pins holding him to the table. Then she placed him on the grass at our feet and we waited. After a moment's pause, Cyndie took her bare toe and prodded him in the rear for encouragement. Mr. Frog took one hop that day— just one.

Mama was furious. It was obvious we hadn't learned anything from the bumblebee episode. She said we were supposed to take care of God's creatures, not harm them, and then she showed us in the Bible where it says God feeds the ravens and knows when the sparrows fall to the ground. I felt bad for what we'd done to His frog.

Shellie Rushing Tomlinson

Cyn-Cyn the R.N., that's what we call her today. It's true what they say; "Everyone has to start somewhere".

Are not two sparrows sold for four cents? And not one of them shall fall on the ground without your Father knowing. Matthew 10:29

LESSON NUMBER ELEVEN
"Trolleys, They're all they're cracked up to be"

Mama taught us to treat others the way we would like to be treated...

Come to think of it, maybe Cyndie got her doctoring skills from Papa. There was that incident with my arm that earned him the nickname of Doctor Rushing. It happened the year Rhonda went to kindergarten. Suddenly, my sister club was down to one. At first I was excited about having Mama to myself. Then I got bored. I couldn't wait for Cyndie and Rhonda to get home. By early afternoon you could find me waiting for them at the carport door. When the bus lumbered near, I'd run to meet them at the end of the driveway and carry their books inside.

One day I was late getting outside when I heard the bus rolling to a stop in the loose gravel. Out the door I flew, speeding down the drive as fast as I could. I hadn't made it very far when my legs got tangled, and by the time I rolled to a painful stop, my knees and elbows were skinned up and bruised, and my right arm was hurting something fierce. I didn't like doctors anymore than Papa did. I kept that arm tucked into my body for a week or so and went about my business. Mama was worried it might be broken. Papa turned it this way and that and after making sure I could flex my fingers open and closed he confidently pronounced it bruised. At the end of the week Cyndie and Rhonda got tired of helping me button my pants and told Mama that I couldn't do it by myself. She took me to town immediately. Doctor Frank A. Cain looked at my arm and said,

"When in the *~!#$%^ did Ed Rushing become a doctor? This baby's arm has been broken for a week!"

Once we got home Mama gave Doctor Rushing a hard time because it really wasn't his first misdiagnosis. Papa never did like to "run to a doctor every time someone stubbed his toe". In his defense, I have to say; we often found creative ways to hurt ourselves.

46

Shellie Rushing Tomlinson

Like the time I had my first electricity lesson. We'd had company over for supper. It was a humid summer evening. The adults were drinking coffee in the living room and we kids were playing hide and seek inside with a little metal ring. Everything was fine until it came my turn to hide the ring. I wanted to find the very best place; when I saw the cord to the radio, I thought I'd found it. I unplugged the cord and put the ring on its prongs before attempting to plug it back in the socket. I remember a very loud noise and a puff of black smoke before the lights flickered; and I remember Mama fussing at Doctor Rushing for laughing while he examined me.

In my defense, not all of my accidents were my fault. Take the time Cyndie and Rhonda tried to kill me on the trolley. Okay, maybe that's a little strong, but they definitely tried to hurt me.

I don't suppose everyone has ridden a trolley, so I'll set this story up for you. My sisters and I built a lot of trolleys in our time. They're fairly simple to make. First, you need a good strong rope (a cable actually), and a length of pipe a little larger in diameter than the rope. One of our first trolleys was built in Papa's equipment shed. We attached a length of twine to the pipe and threaded the pipe onto the cable before anchoring one end of the cable to the loft upstairs and the other end to a pole about five feet from the ground. We used the twine to pull the pipe up the rope as we climbed the ladder to the loft.

Once the construction was finished, it was time for the real fun. Riding the trolley was simple—we wrapped our fingers around the pipe and hung from our hands as the pipe slid down the rope. (Trolley riding gives you a nice shoulder stretch.) The only thing you really needed to remember was to let go and drop to the ground before you reached the pole at the bottom. By nature of their design, some of our trolleys were more exciting than others were; which brings me to the point of my story...

One day Cyndie and Rhonda came looking for me, excited about the improvements they'd made in our latest trolley. As anchors for this ride we'd used the trees beside the house, tying one end high at the top of a great old oak and the other on the lowest limb of a tree about thirty feet away. It looked exactly the same to me as it had when we originally built it, but they both insisted it was twice as much fun.

Lessons Learned on Bull Run Road

Rhonda's eyes should've been my first clue that something was up; she looked like she'd been crying. But being the gullible baby sister I climbed the tree and got ready to ride. Cyndie hollered up at me to make sure that I pushed extra hard off the tree so I could get up some speed. Little did I know additional force was unnecessary, nor did I know that Cyndie had taken Papa's grease gun and greased the rope and the inside of the pipe! As a result, the amount of time a person had to judge her distance and drop to the ground safely before meeting the second tree was greatly reduced. Unfortunately, I wasn't privy to any of this information.

I clasped the trolley, placed one foot on the nearest limb, and pushed away from the tree trunk violently with the other foot. I don't remember much about the ride down other than it was extremely fast. I do remember my impact with the tree at the bottom. Back then I wore round "hoot owl" glasses. When Mama was summoned for medical aid, she found me lying on my back with one half of my glasses to my right and the other half to my left. Cyndie and Rhonda were both in deep trouble. Mama was especially disappointed in Rhonda because Cyndie had tricked her into riding the trolley before I did, and she still acted as an accomplice. When Mama got through with them, my sisters offered to help me tape up my glasses.

Therefore all things whatsoever you would that men should do to you, do you even so to them. Matthew 7:12

LESSON NUMBER TWELVE
"Work Hard, Play Harder"

A philosopher once said that no man is an island. The people of Melbourne Community taught me how special it was to be a part of something larger than yourself...

Reading about today's latchkey kids makes my heart ache. For many of these children, adults are only shadowy figures on the perimeter of their lives. These kids move in parallel lines with busy parents who are working longer and harder just to make ends meet. At school, they are faces in the crowd and in the afternoons they come home to empty houses, spending most of their time alone or with other children. I don't believe most parents are choosing this lifestyle. I think they're caught in a tug of war between a desire to spend time with their kids and a need to keep their job. Unfortunately, that doesn't change the hard facts. More and more children are set adrift in an adult world long before they have their bearings.

There was a time when I wouldn't have seen this as a problem; the people of Melbourne took the concept of community involvement to a whole new level. Growing up in that tight knit group of families on Highway 65 meant having a network of adults attending to our "learning". We were taught respect for our elders—all of them. There were aunts, uncles, Sunday school teachers, preachers and family friends, an endless supply of grownups with our best interests at heart. My sisters and I considered this a major liability.

Mama knew everything we did before we did it, and she'd never reveal her source, telling us only that a "little bird" told her. This galled us more than the spankings. You could count on—if we got into trouble at school, that anonymous bird was singing to Mama before we got off the bus. We girls used to fantasize about clipping that bird's beak!

As frustrating as all this togetherness could be, it had its good points—I never knew lonely as a child. At any time of any day I could find an available

Lessons Learned on Bull Run Road

lap for loving or a ready ear for listening. But in my memory, one of the biggest benefits of having this overextended "family" were the trips we took together during the summer. By "we" I mean practically the whole community. Think of it as double the people, double the pleasure and double the fun.

These vacations were well deserved. With very few exceptions our daddies all made their living farming. My Uncle Byron said it best with a poem he once wrote called "The Gambling Man". This poem didn't have anything to do with casinos. Instead it told how Papa and the other men would hold their breath and roll the dice every year, hoping against hope that their fortunes were about to change, regardless of how Lady Luck had cheated them in the past. And each spring they'd turn their backs on their past losses to plant a little more of their hearts along with their seed.

The land is a hard taskmaster. By summer's end, when the crops were tall and independent, and whatever was going to happen had already been written in the ground, and our mamas had planned and pleaded—our daddies could be talked into taking a break. They knew how to work hard; and they knew how to play hard.

A destination would be chosen in advance, though reservations were seldom made, and early on the appointed morning we'd all pull out together in one big convoy: cars and trucks, stationwagons and campers. Over the years we saw the mountains and the beaches and everything in between.

At lunchtime our caravan would stop at a rest area and pull out the hampers and coolers stocked with bread and lunchmeat, sodas and chips. After lunch we kids were allowed to run around and stretch our legs. We rarely finished a full meal; the fuel from our pent up excitement charged our batteries and kept us in constant motion. They say times have changed and this could be a good example. Odds are, if we were kids today, most of us would be medicated.

We kids used these rest stops as an opportunity to play musical cars. As long as the head count was correct, no one paid much attention to who had whose children. Hours later we'd descend on an unsuspecting hotel like a band of gypsies in a bad western. I don't know how they ever found a place willing to take us all. We kids would bounce around inside the cars while a couple of men would go "check out" the place. A tour of the pool area was always a top priority as it was destined to be the main casualty of our assault. (It has just occurred to me that there could have been another reason we were left in the car—to increase the chance of getting the rooms!)

One time we were leaving Texas with Papa guiding the caravan down the interstate, when a radio spot about Freddy Fender came on—the singer was appearing at the Texas Stadium that very evening and there were tickets at the door. Papa loved Mr. Fender's hit song "I'll be there Before the Next Tear Drop Falls." A quick poll on the CB radio garnered enough support for an itinerary change. Neither the caravan headed in the wrong direction, nor the absence of an exit proved a strong deterrent for Papa. He took a U-turn through the medium and out into the lanes of traffic traveling in the opposite direction with Mama hollering all the while,

"Ed, you're gonna get everybody killed!"

I remember turning around in the back seat and watching seven or eight vehicles follow the leader.

Behold that which I have seen: it is good and comely for one to eat and to drink, and to enjoy the good of all his labor that he takes under the sun all the days of his life which God gives him: for this is his portion. Ecclesiastes 5:18-19

LESSON NUMBER THIRTEEN
"Tag Team Preaching"

My sisters and I spent a lot of time at church, and not necessarily organized services. I learned that Faith is a strong foundation to build a life on...

I can't remember not being aware of God. One of my earliest memories is of riding my bike down the road and singing my own made up songs to the Lord. My sisters and I grew up in the pews of Melbourne Baptist Church. There were Sundays and Wednesdays, one revival in the spring and one in the fall, cottage prayer meetings before each, and always Vacation Bible School—which was just like church, but with crafts and Kool-Aid. You also got to wear shorts to Vacation Bible School and once you got to the big kid department, you could carry the flags in the opening processional. There were the American Flag, the Christian Flag and the Salute to the Bible—we celebrated each and every morning, singing songs in their honor. Afterwards we learned the stories of the Bible and made our own golden treasure chests (cigar boxes with dry macaroni glued to the top and sprayed with gold paint). At the end of the week we'd put on a program for our parents and once we were through, they'd tour our classrooms and examine our workmanship.

One summer a missionary from Africa came to hold our summer revival. He showed us slides from the deep, dark jungles and told us stories of demon-possessed natives. Cyndie and Rhonda and I had never heard anything like this. We listened with round eyes and open mouths as the missionary told how one of the natives began speaking in different voices and cutting himself as the demon inside the man threw him around the hut. When the native was asked directly, "To whom are we speaking?" A low voice answered, "Meeebbaaaaaaaa, we are many."

Much later that night we went home with the missionary's stories circling in our heads. While Cyndie was brushing her teeth, Rhonda managed to sneak under her bed. She waited patiently for Cyndie to come in, turn out the lights and get under the covers. Just when Cyndie was about to drift off—Rhonda chanted in a low voice,

"Meeeeebbaaaaaaa"

Rhonda got a beating and a lecture, in that order. The beating came from Cyndie before Papa broke it up for the lecture.

While it's true that we went to church a lot, it was my Papaw Stone's church members who were the experts at endurance. Papaw Stone, my mother's dad, pastored a small church in Natchez, Mississippi. Papaw Stone was a long-winded, old-fashioned, "fire and brimstone" Southern Baptist preacher...and my hero. He was larger than life to us grandkids. We took our front row seats and watched him weep, laugh, rebuke and encourage his people with the truth of God's word, written in his well-worn Bible and in his enormous heart. As a little kid I just knew he and the Good Lord were so close, that whatever God knew he probably told Papaw. This one thought might have saved me a spanking or two while I was in Natchez.

From my earliest memory Papaw Stone pastored Riverside Baptist Church and raised his family in the parsonage next door. During the singing and announcements, he sat on stage in a big wooden chair with a thick green velvet cushion. In my eyes that chair was huge. Whenever I heard about God sitting on the throne, I pictured Papaw in his chair. And to this day when someone mentions the Great White Throne of Judgment, my mind goes back to that chair and Riverside Baptist Church.

Papaw Stone wouldn't put up with much talking from his parishioner's children and even less from his own grandkids. He tended to call us out as examples. Sometimes we got too noisy and caught Papaw's attention while he was preaching. It was always a shock to hear your name inserted into his sermon.

"The Bible says—*Shellie, you and Lisa put the paper away and be quiet*—to love one another."

And heaven forbid you didn't heed Papaw's first warning! For he was all business on the second one.

"Shellie baby, now you come on up here so you can behave."

53

Lessons Learned on Bull Run Road

He said this like he was doing you a favor! I'd have to sit there in his chair the remainder of the service, facing the congregation with my black patent feet sticking straight out.

It was here at Riverside that we were first introduced to all night prayer meetings. (That's what the adults called them. I remember it as tag-team preaching.) When one preacher would run out of gas, he'd tag another one. This process could go on for hours. In and around all this preaching there was special music and breaks when everyone would head to the fellowship hall for refreshments.

With all this churchin' you might think we kids would be burnt out on the idea. Wrong! We weren't supposed to play in Papaw's church, but if the cat were away, we mice would slip in and it would be Sunday morning all over again. Rhonda would play the piano and Cyndie would lead the singing and make announcements. Cousin Lisa would occupy a pew until it was time to take up the offering. Me, I liked to be the preacher as often as they would let me. Papaw had a wooden pulpit with three shelves on the inside. I would climb to the top shelf in order to lean over the pulpit and pound it like Papaw while giving my message. I was loud and to the point. My listeners needed to turn from their wicked ways and follow the Lord while there was time. But for the grace of God, I would explain, they could die that very night and burn in hell. At the close of my message, we expected our youngest cousins, Michelle and Jeff, to come down front and repent. Sometimes it took several hard stares from Cyndie as she led the altar call, before they realized they were sorry for their many sins.

Now faith is the assurance of things hoped for, the evidence of things not seen. Hebrews 11:1

LESSON NUMBER FOURTEEN
"Reverend Marvin Stone and the African Mongoose"

Papaw taught us to balance our lives with a good sense of humor. He lived by the creed: laugh, and the world laughs with you...

Mama had three sisters and one brother. Elaine was the oldest. Mama was next in line and then Aunt Marleta, Aunt Judy and Rodney. The two oldest girls were married and Mama was pregnant with Cyndie when Grandmaw found out about Rodney. At first she thought she was going through the change. At the doctor's office they assured her that things were just beginning to change. Grandmaw was mad when she got home—but Papaw was thrilled! She called him a foolish old man and threatened to throw the supper dishes at him. It took a good bit of charming and teasing from Papaw, but eventually he had her laughing too.

The Stones were a close family and Mama couldn't go long without loading us up for the two-hour trip back to Natchez. We didn't watch television much at home; Mama hated to see us inside on a pretty day. We didn't watch it at all in Natchez. Papaw and Grandmaw Stone did have a TV once, but Papaw turned it on and saw something offensive one too many times. Having as he did a low boiling point for the devil's doings, he picked up that TV set and threw it right out into the back yard, where it stayed for a long time. I don't know who finally picked it up and carried it off. Papaw had threatened to do this before, but Grandmaw could usually talk him out of it, "for the kids." Papaw killed it for the same reason, "the kids".

That was my Papaw for you. He had a lot of simple solutions. Take our tennis shoes for example. Our feet always seemed to outgrow our shoes about the time we'd come to stay a week or two in Natchez. Papaw would take his pocketknife and cut the toe boxes out of everyone's sneakers, providing us with both ample toe room and sole protection, a neat fad that never caught on.

Papaw loved people—all colors, shapes and sizes. He loved to preach at 'em, pray with 'em, and help 'em any way he could. During my summer visits I

55

Lessons Learned on Bull Run Road

looked forward to Saturdays and street preaching with Papaw. He'd always try to talk me out of going, knowing full well that I was going to get hot and thirsty and want to come home a long time before he finished sharing the word. But I'd put up a fuss and Papaw would end up letting me tag along.

Once we were situated on the street corner, he'd begin to tell the world that Jesus loved them. It bothered me that some people stopped to listen, and some people practically walked over us; but Papaw didn't care. He was happiest when he was preaching. "My part is just planting," he'd say. "The harvest is the Lord's business." For a little while I'd be happy just being with my Papaw and watching the people come and go, determined to prove to both of us that I could last as long as he could. But it was usually only a matter of time before his prophecy came to pass.

Papaw and I had our own little routine. As a reward for good behavior, I always got to buy one coke from the little grocery on the corner. I'd sit on that concrete and wait as long as I could, knowing in my heart that once I had my treat Papaw was going to get his second wind. When I thought I couldn't stand it any longer, I'd tug at the pocket of his trousers. Without pausing in his preaching, Papaw would reach in and pull out a couple of coins for me. I'd hold the ice-cold bottle against my forehead before sipping the brown stuff slowly, letting it burn good all the way down.

Papaw Stone was almost as fond of playing tricks on people as he was at preaching to them. He had jokes for every occasion, but his favorite prank involved the African Mongoose.

Papaw would turn into a little kid when he found someone who had never seen his mongoose. He'd take the wooden box from the back of his pickup and begin his story. Seems he got this African mongoose from a missionary friend that brought him back from the jungle. Papaw kept it in a box that was probably four feet long and a foot high. One end of the box was boarded up except for a small opening that led into the other end, which was enclosed with chicken wire. At this small opening of the enclosed end you could glimpse a couple of strands of long black hair from the elusive animal, (which was actually a wig from Aunt Marletta's beauty shop). Papaw had the top of the small house spring-loaded. He could let if fly open with a touch of his finger. Unbeknown to his audience, there was a second wig attached to the lid—ready to fly through the air and in the direction of the unsuspecting soul at the wrong end of the box.

As the joke progressed, Papaw would describe in vivid detail the long claws and sharp teeth of the mongoose. He'd bemoan the fact that the little animal was so vicious that he'd never been able to let him out in all the years he had him. Why once, he would remember, the little thing got out accidentally and tore all the hide off of his old coon dog. Papaw would shake his head sadly. That dog hadn't treed a coon since. Papaw would make a big show of banging on the side of the box and trying to get the thing to come out, all the while reminding his captive audience to be really careful of the lid. When he was sure he had a couple of victims lined up just right, he'd flip the switch and watch the fun as the wig flew out of the box and attacked his victims. Although we kids saw this show countless times, it never failed to send us into fits of laughter. That African mongoose could tree a grown man faster than a good dog could tree a coon.

A merry heart does good like a medicine, but a broken spirit dries the bones. Proverbs 17:22

LESSON NUMBER FIFTEEN
"Rival Gangs and Hobos"

My sisters and I were taught to respect everyone, regardless of his or her station in life...

A big red hill stood directly behind my grandparents' house, perfect for sliding down in empty cardboard boxes. Grandmaw fumed about the ruddy soil that left tenacious stains on our clothes and tinted our skin a faint pink, no matter how hard we scrubbed. As we got older the stand of woods behind the hill beckoned to us. The oldest cousins went the furthest into the woods on their explorations, even finding a little pond to claim as their own. Cyndie let me go with her once all the way to their hideout. It felt like we were the only people ever to walk in those woods.

There were several gangs of us cousins when we all got together in Natchez but the oldest gang ruled—it was comprised of Rod, Steve and Cyndie. I found my mischief with the middle gang, Rhonda and Lisa as my allies. At the bottom of the totem pole, Jeff and Michelle struggled for respect. And then there was Little Stan, who had the misfortune of being too young for the old gang, too old for the young gang and too male for the middle gang. Life was hard for Little Stan. Some days he forced himself into one of the gangs, but for the most part he shunned us all and played with the dogs.

One day Lisa and Rhonda and I went looking for Little Stan. I don't remember why; but if I had to guess, I'd say we needed a judge. Like true Southern girls, we liked to stage beauty pageants, complete with talent and swimsuit divisions. Generally we contestants each cast a vote. Rhonda won more often than anyone else did. Lisa and I got tired of it—but we still voted for her. Sometimes we went looking for an outside judge, which beings me back to my story...

We couldn't find Little Stan anywhere. Grandma Stone said he wasn't inside, and we weren't going to be either. The young gang didn't have a clue, but they were willing to join the search party. We expected as much from them, but it was the oldest gang we found suspiciously helpful. They hadn't seen Little Stan all afternoon, or so they said.

It happened that we found our missing cousin tied to a tree in the woods far behind the church beside a small pond—he'd been pestering the wrong crowd. Cyndie, Rod, and Steve were very repentant as they pleaded with Grandmaw for leniency. Their defense was full of holes: they never intended to leave him out there, it was a joke—ha, ha? Grandma delivered them to Papaw for sentencing and they served hard time for kidnapping.

After supper we kids were allowed to go back outside. Grandmaw would turn on the porch light and we'd play until bedtime or the mosquitoes chased us in, whichever came first. One night Rhonda and Lisa and I were jumping rope in front of the house when an old hobo staggered into Papaw's yard. We hadn't seen him coming, and he scared us. We screamed and ran inside for the adults. Grandma invited the man in and fed him while Papaw rounded him up a clean change of clothes. A good while later the old guy left, but not before Papaw told him about the Lord and gave him all the money in his pockets.

Rhonda and Lisa and I were bathed and cleansed of the day's red dirt, tucked in a double bed and giggling in the dark when Papaw came to find us. He sat on the edge of our bed and told us how the old hobo had feelings just like anyone else, and we had no idea what had happened in the man's life to bring him to where he was now. It was right to come inside, he told us, but wrong to embarrass the man by screaming and running from him. He told us that in God's eyes the man was special, just like us. That night Papaw taught us about human dignity and respect.

My grandfather didn't have to tell us kids he loved people; we saw him loving them every day. One of the biggest reasons we weren't supposed to play in his church was because drifters often slipped in at night, looking for a place to lay their head. Papaw didn't want us around them, just in case they were dangerous. But if he found them, he'd see to their basic needs first. (Papaw said a man couldn't think about heavenly things with his stomach growling.) Before long the two of them would be joking and laughing like they were old friends. Then my Papaw would offer them an eternal answer.

Lessons Learned on Bull Run Road

Papaw used to stop for hitchhikers, too, even though everyone warned him not to. Of course, the world wasn't quite as dangerous back then, but there was still cause for concern. Grandmaw was fully against this policy; she fussed at him about it all the time, but she never changed his mind. I remember Papaw saying that he couldn't and wouldn't pass someone in need, and if that led to him getting robbed or worse, well that was the Lord's business. Then he'd smile and wave as he drove off. I'd watch him and hope the Lord was paying attention.

My brethren have not the faith of our Lord Jesus Christ, the Lord of glory, with respect of persons. James 2:1

LESSON NUMBER SIXTEEN
"How to Pack Cotton"

Living in a farming community, my sisters and I saw our share of farming related accidents and deaths. I came to understand that while the body might be fragile, the God given spirit of man is anything but—and the fate of both rest in His hands...

Delta summers are long, hot and dry. They only begin to end when you can't remember anything else. One morning you wake up and the air smells different, cleaner somehow; and it nips at your bare arms. The days begin to shorten, and all the signs point to the harvest. That's when the farmers roll out the cottonpickers and combines, blow them off, oil them up, and unleash them on the heavily-laden fields.

Papa would let us pack cotton for him in the evening when we got home from school. The bus would barely roll to a stop before we were in our rooms racing to change into play clothes and meet Papa in the field.

The closer we got to the tall cotton trailers, the stronger the familiar smells became. Even now, it's hard for me to distinguish between the strong woodsy smell of cotton in my memory and the bitter smell of stinkbugs. These little green bugs leave a disagreeable odor wherever they walk. And if you fool around and squash a stinkbug—the smell intensifies. Because stinkbugs love cotton, the two are inseparable at harvest time.

When the basket on the cottonpicker filled up, Papa would dump his load of white, fluffy cotton into the trailer and ramble off quickly so the big machine could eat up as much cotton as possible before the sun began its descent and the rising moisture signaled the day's end. Meanwhile, Cyndie, Rhonda and I would stay in the trailer to stomp the cotton.

There are at least two ways to "stomp" or "pack" cotton, but only one purpose—to allow more cotton into the trailer and thus fewer trips to the cotton gin in order not to slow down the harvest. The adult labor stomped around in a

Lessons Learned on Bull Run Road

slow, methodical pattern until the cotton was conquered. Our way was much more fun. We'd climb onto the sides of the trailer and jump, dive and fall into the white stuff over and over. In this raw state, cotton isn't all soft and cuddly. Instead, it's strewn with the scratchy brown husks that once held the individual cotton boles on the plant. We wore blue jeans and long sleeves when we packed to avoid the itchy scrapes of these husks. While we played we were obligated to keep an eye out for Papa. If his cottonpicker were close to filling up again, we went into serious stomping mode so as not to slow him down when he came around to dump another load.

We loved to dig tunnels in the cotton. We were experts at packing and forming the stretchy white stuff into a maze of tunnels beneath the visible top layer. The tunnels scared Papa and Mama and were only allowed under certain conditions. You could never, ever play in the cotton by yourself, and we could never under any circumstances dig tunnels while the trailer was in the field. Mama had known a little boy who fell asleep and suffocated in his bed of cotton because his dad dumped a fresh load on him without knowing he was there. Only when Papa stored a trailer overnight under the shed could we create our white wonderland.

There is a small window of opportunity to harvest a crop, and sometimes haste edges out caution. It wasn't rare to hear of someone losing a finger or hand to the big machinery. Just about everyone knew someone who had been maimed or killed in a harvest-related accident. Sometimes a load of cotton would begin to smolder, bursting into flames in the steel basket of the cottonpicker while the unsuspecting driver continued down the field.

I remember my own harvest accident. We'd been playing hard for hours, and I was taking a breather perched on the top of the cotton trailer. I lost my balance and fell backward onto the hard-packed road. Cyndie and Rhonda climbed down quickly, sure I was dead or dying. They only began to laugh once the breath came back into my body and they felt confident I would live.

It's impossible to talk about harvest accidents without mentioning Neil. Have I told you about the Horath kids? There were four girls and one boy in their family. That was Neal; he was the baby. He also had nine lives.

Shellie Rushing Tomlinson

One day Papa came home white as a sheet. He told Mama he'd just finished helping some of the other men cut Mr. Al Horath's little boy, Neil, out of a the teeth of a combine. Neil was two at the time. His daddy had been working on a combine at the shed behind their house. He thought Neil was inside with his mother. His mother thought their little boy was inside, too. Neil was outside.

Against all odds Neil lived, although he was in a full body cast for months. When he got a little better, his daddy made him a little dolly to get around on, similar to the type mechanics use to roll under cars. Neil would lay on his belly and use his hands to roll himself around.

Several years later Neil was at a class swimming party in town. All the kids were inside eating cake and ice cream when someone decided to count heads. They found Neil at the bottom of the pool, blue and lifeless. Neil was resuscitated that day and taken to the hospital, again. The doctors worried about brain damage because of the lack of oxygen. Neil made a full recovery.

Neil is a policeman now in Tallulah, La. A couple of years ago he was involved in a high-speed chase. My father-in-law and his drug-searching dogs often work with the same department. He saw Neil flip his cruiser end over end for what seemed like an eternity. Many people were amazed that Neil survived—we weren't.

To every thing there is a season, and a time to every purpose under the heaven: a time to be born and a time to die. Ecclesiastes 2:1-2

LESSON NUMBER SEVENTEEN
"My Crash Course in Tractor Driving"

Papa often showed us the power of a word to diffuse or ignite a tense situation...

Mama didn't like to see us girls fight. We solved this by making sure she wasn't looking. One day she went grocery shopping and left us home alone. Papa was working on his equipment in the shed. Cyndie was in one of her famous pestering moods and she'd been trying to get a rise out of Rhonda all day. I finally got tired of hearing Rhonda whining and decided to intervene.

"Leave her alone," I told Cyndie.

Cyndie was shocked—this was a first. "Oh, and what are you going to do if I don't?" she taunted, sauntering slowly behind my chair as if she was headed to the kitchen. This made me uneasy. I was fully prone in Papa's blue recliner and at a distinct disadvantage. Just as I was trying to get in a better defensive position, she attacked, grabbing me around the neck and commencing to give me a "noogie". A "noogie" means to take your knuckles and rub them back and forth quickly in the top of someone's head, like you're trying to start a fire. Receiving a noogie is more of an assault to your pride than it is to your person. What happened next was the classic example of the scene where the good hearted underdog gets up his nerve to confront the bully.

I back flipped out of the recliner and onto Cyndie's head. Ding! Ding! Round one! We rolled and punched and fought our way from the living room to the kitchen with Rhonda providing the sound effects. Cyndie would roll on top of me and hit my head against the refrigerator, and then I'd roll on top of her and hit her head on the stove. Rhonda was sure someone was going to get killed. She screamed this at the top of her lungs during the entire brawl.

Cyndie and I were deep in the middle of round two when we heard the door slam shut. We froze with loaded fists and looked up to find Papa standing there with his hands on his hips. We were sure we were going to get it. But all Papa said was "Boy, I wish I'd seen that one!"

Of course, he had to tell Mama. I guess it was in their parent pact or something. She wasn't pleased with us for fighting, and she wasn't pleased with Papa and how he had addressed it. On the other hand, we girls liked the way he handled it. Papa had a way of doing that—letting you off the hook. It was one of my first looks at grace; what the Bible calls unmerited favor. I saw it again later that fall.

Once the crops were harvested it was time to plow the fields before they were left vacant for the winter months. Cyndie learned to drive a tractor early; a skill Rhonda and I tried to avoid since all it had gotten Cyndie was a lot of extra field time. Then one day I took a crash course.

Papa was just finishing some maintenance on his tractor when I happened by on my way to the basketball goal. He caught a quick glimpse of me out of the corner of his eye.

"Cyndie," he said, "get on this tractor and follow me around the shed and help me hook up to the planter. "

Well, I tried to explain that I wasn't Cyndie, but he cut me off gruffly and stormed in the direction of the shed. You have to understand, when Papa was working hard he stayed wound pretty tight. Given the opportunity I would've explained that I didn't know how to drive a tractor. Instead I climbed aboard and looked around. I'd ridden with Papa enough to know how to crank it up. I even managed to follow him in first gear. *Well, would you look at this,* I thought, *I am a tractor driver.* My pleasure was short lived.

As we pulled up beside the shed, Papa hollered at me to stop. Unfortunately, this was the first time I looked for the brake. I found two of them! Did I know the left brake stopped the left wheel and the right brake stopped the right wheel, and unless you pressed them both the tractor would take a hard turn in the direction of whichever one you chose? No! I simply chose the one on the left and hit it hard. Unfortunately, that was the same side the shed was on. One loud crash later, I held my breath and met Papa's surprised eyes. After an eternity he began to chuckle.

65

Lessons Learned on Bull Run Road

"Shellie Charlene," he asked, holding his side and laughing, "what are you doing up there? You don't know how to drive a tractor!" He took the words right out of my mouth.

A man hath joy by the answer of his mouth: and a word spoken in due season, how good it is. Proverbs 15:23

LESSON NUMBER EIGHTEEN
"Rodney Comes to Rule"

Growing up on Bull Run Road afforded us plenty of opportunities to learn the art of compromise…

I'm not sure how she hit on this plan but Mama had a sure-fire way of ending our disagreements. When we were little and she found us fighting, she'd make the two warring parties sit together under the dining room table. And there we would remain—cross-legged and furious, with the chairs pushed in around us, while Mama went about her business.

It was hard to stay mad under the table. For one thing it was ridiculous—and we both knew it. And sometimes from our holding cell we could see our other sister watching cartoons and eating cookies, (slyly supplied by the warden), while we were under the table with no chance of parole unless we kissed and made up.

Before very long someone would break down and have to giggle, and the fight would be over, just like that. We'd be on the same side again, except for the kissing thing. We always hated that, but the warden required it. One day Rhonda and I even went back in the lockup and played Barbie under the table. Ken and his wife (they were always married) had inherited a mansion with a lot of different rooms (beneath the chairs) and a couple of floors (on the seat of the chairs).

Actually, I think Mama was on to something. I bet the world would be a better place if everyone had to sit under a table with their arms around their enemy's neck until they got along.

As we grew older the things we fought over evolved with us, especially after Rodney moved in. Rodney Ryle Stone, we called him Rod, was Mama's younger brother. He came to live with us for good when he was seventeen after spending several prior summers working in the field for Papa. Rod didn't like school, so he decided to test out early and get on to what he did like—farming.

67

Lessons Learned on Bull Run Road

I thought we were getting the older brother I'd always wanted. Rod thought it was his duty to protect us and be our boss. There's a saying in the South, "the fur flew". Although it originally referred to a catfight, it appropriately describes the clash that followed Rod's self-appointed guardianship.

One hot summer evening when I was about thirteen, I wandered out to the shed to call Papa to supper. I found him welding three seats on a strange new apparatus he'd attached to the front of a tractor. Beside each seat was a spray wand. This wand was connected to a hose that led to a large tank of chemicals mounted on the front of the tractor.

Papa said it was a new ride, a lot like Six Flags. The next morning, starting at six o'clock, and for the next couple of weeks afterwards, we got up to ride Papa's new invention. Six Flags this was not! Rodney got to drive; Cyndie, Rhonda and I resentfully took the three seats. Up and down the field we went, pointing our little sprayers at the Johnson grass we passed and giving it a little squirt of chemical. We passed the time singing to the tractor's radio while Rod pointed out every single blade of grass we missed. Tensions began to mount.

Late one afternoon we girls were standing on the footrests Papa had kindly supplied beneath our seats, rocking to the radio and using our spray wands as imaginary guitars. Rod was having a major fit as he watched us pass weed after weed. Taking it upon himself to teach us a lesson, he hit the brakes hard, sending us flying off into the cotton. We came up dirty, skinned and mad. After a lot of squabbling our unhappy rig resumed its trip down the field. But we three sisters had formed a plan.

On the count of three, we turned on our bossy driver and doused him good with a heavy dose of chemicals. We caught the devil from Papa for wasting the expensive chemicals and more grief from Mama because it was poisonous—but revenge was still sweet.

To Rod's credit he was a quick study; and the main shut off valve was at his fingertips. After that he was quick on the switch at the first sign of mutiny. He had a problem though; if he left it off we couldn't spray the weeds. Since this bothered him a lot more than it did us we finished the job under an uneasy truce.

Shellie Rushing Tomlinson

The beginning of strife is as when one lets out water; therefore leave off strife before it is meddled with. Proverbs 17-14

LESSON NUMER NINETEEN
"Papa's Pedicure"

Papa and Mama might have taught us the ways of the Lord, but I know we helped them learn patience...

As my sisters and I grew up our interests changed and we began to notice boys for something other than fighting. Papa didn't like this much at all. No one was good enough for his girls. Our experiences with Papa took off in a new direction.

Some of the kids at school used to brag about sneaking out of their houses. This is one crime that wasn't on our record. All of the boys called our house *Alcatraz,* after the famous prison. The word was, our house was impossible to break into or out of. I felt duty bound to prove them wrong. One night I hatched an escape plan with two of my friends as witnesses; at stake was a five-dollar bill.

As soon as everyone was fast asleep, I slipped out of my window and met the guys on the road down from our house. I quickly pocketed the money and took off—feeling as I did that the timing of my mission was crucial.

Back at *Alcatraz* I eased the window open and started to climb in. This is when my plan threatened to fall apart, for I had overlooked a couple of crucial details. First, since I shared a bedroom with Rhonda, I really shouldn't have left her out of the loop. And second, I should've tied the sheers away from the window on my way out. For just as I stepped back inside the floor length window with my hands stretched out in front of me, feeling for the center opening of the fabric panels—Rhonda woke up and rolled over, only to see those see-through white sheers flowing around my body like a ghostly shroud.

By the time Papa made it to our room, I'd slipped under the covers and threatened to choke my roommate if she didn't stop yelling. When the door opened I rubbed my eyes against the hall light and murmured something about

Rhonda having a bad nightmare. Beside me she lay quivering and sobbing into her pillow. Miraculously, the community canary never sang of my adventure. Actually, Rhonda wasn't the only one to suffer with nightmares; we must have given Papa and Mama plenty over the next few years. One day Papa came in from the field, ate one of Mama's good meals, stretched out on the sofa and fell into a deep sleep. He had taken off his socks and shoes and his bare white feet shone like beacons. We girls couldn't help but notice the bottle of red fingernail polish sitting on the coffee table beside him. It was a natural progression.

Papa began to stir as we worked on the last few toes and we manicurists scattered like chickens running from a chicken hawk. I don't know if Papa was madder at us for painting or at Mama for letting us paint. He hated the smell of fingernail polish remover. It made him sick. He refused to use it—opting for it to wear off instead. For the next few weeks we tried not to laugh when Papa got out of the shower at night and plodded around the house barefoot with his beautifully manicured toes. Eventually though, he laughed with us.

Almost every night Papa would call us into his and Mama's room where we'd all pile onto their bed for our family prayer time. One night after Papa finished the devotion we stayed a little while longer, visiting before everyone turned in. For some unknown reason we got it in our heads that Papa should let us put one of Cyndie's hard contact lens in his eye—so he could see what it was like. Mama registered her opinion early; she didn't think it was a good idea.

We had barely got it into his eye before Papa agreed with her. The contact began to cut his eye, and he began to holler. He wanted it out already, but because of the pain he couldn't open his eye for us to remove it. He yelled at us to get it out, and we yelled at him to open his eye. Mama yelled at everyone. We girls finally managed to pry his eye open and remove the offending lens. Papa's eye was read and swollen; and once the excitement was over, the whole thing struck us as extremely funny. For a minute or two it was hard to tell if Papa was laughing or crying. And for the record: he hasn't worn contacts since.

In your patience possess you your soul. Luke 21:19

LESSON NUMBER TWENTY
"Full Circle"

One lesson from my childhood stands out above all others. When everything is said and done, it is love that endures...

I look outside as dusk falls and the streetlights begin to glow, preparing to take the night shift. My teenagers should be home soon. Standing here at the screen door I am acutely aware of Time's steady march. The scene before me fades and voices and faces from the past come into focus...

Inside my grandparent's house, on a little country road in Natchez, Mississippi, my mother is visiting with family and friends. Light spills from the open windows and into the yard where my cousins and I are playing. The sounds of their laughter floats through well-worn screens, southern necessities we rely on to let the air in and keep the mosquitoes out. The grownups are retelling cherished childhood stories, their voices providing a sheltering backdrop that is our anchor. We're making our own memories, delighted that dusk has given way to night and no one has called us in.

A challenge has been issued. It is a game of fear and false bravado and the cousins line up by age, eldest first. The dare before us: who can run the deepest into the graveyard lying next to Papaw's church? To play you must touch the farthest tombstone you can reach before the fear that renders you breathless propels you safely back to the light. For even the fear—as strong and gripping as it is—has boundaries. Mounted above the front step of Papaw's church hangs a single light bulb whose warm glow embraces us and banishes all evil. Beneath that light we are safe; only steps from the graveyard but miles from the fear that lives there.

The older cousins are the bravest, urged on by the responsibility of their superior years. Some go the distance, waving from the other end of the graveyard before sauntering back. It seems their saunter gains momentum as they near our precious light, but I dare not say so. My stomach is churning when my time comes and I can feel my legs betraying me before my hand ever reaches a stone. Oh, yes! There is Mama's voice calling us in. Thank you, Lord! I can run without risking the stigma of a scaredy cat. But I want to stay out and play ... She calls again, impatient this time, and I turn...

The screen door bangs shut jolting me back to the present. My teenagers are home. The sweet memories fade, but the smile on my face lingers. It has been said that you can't ever really go home, and this may be true. But now I know that the love nurtured there is never far away. I'll always have the memories of those happy childhood days, whether at my grandparents in Natchez or our family home in Melbourne Community. While it's been years since my sisters and I worked and played on Bull Run Road, the lessons I learned there will be with me always.

Love suffers long, and is kind. Love envies not; does not push itself forward, does not behave unseemly, seeks not her own, is not easily provoked, thinks no evil; rejoices not in iniquity, but rejoices in the truth. Bears all things, believes all things, hopeth all things, endureth all things. Love never fails...and now abideth faith, hope and love; but the greatest of these is love. I Corinthians 13: 4-8, 13

If you enjoyed *Lessons Learned on Bull Run Road* please consider recommending it to a friend.

==

You're invited to subscribe to AllThingsSouthern.com my FREE weekly emag bringing the Charm and Heritage of the South to your email box. To SUBSCRIBE, send a blank email to:
tomtom@allthingssouthern.com
http://www.allthingssouthern.com

==

WHAT SOUTHERN MOMS TELL THEIR DAUGHTERS...A friend's mother gave her this piece of advice on her wedding night: Honey, when you're late with supper, or just plain tired, remember to have the Holy Trinity of Southern cooking (onions, celery and bell pepper) sautéing in a dab of butter or bacon grease when your man comes home--it'll put him in a good mood and you can feed him anything. Shellie Rushing Tomlinson (author of Lessons Learned on Bull Run Road) wants your southern mom's advice about love, marriage, relationships and life in general. Email Shellie, tomtom@allthingssouthern.com, or write to her at Rt. 2 Box 455 Lake Providence, La. 71254 and have your mom's advice memorialized in her new book WHAT SOUTHERN MOMS TELL THEIR DAUGHTERS.

A TASTE OF BULL RUN ROAD
Collected Recipes from Melbourne Community

APPETIZERS, RELISHES AND PICKLES

MELBA RUSHING KING'S FRIED DILL PICKLES

1 egg beaten
1 c. milk
3 ½ c. flour
¾ tsp. Salt

¾ tsp. pepper
1 qt. sliced dill pickles
vegetable oil

Combine milk and egg. Set aside. Mix flour, salt and pepper together. Dip drained pickles into egg mixture, then dip pickles into flour mixture. When pickles are floured well, deep fry in oil until they float and they're golden brown.

DEBBIE TUGGLE'S PARTY PIZZAS

1 lb. sausage (hot)
1 lb. ground beef
1 lb. Velveeta cheese
1 Tbsp. Worcestershire sauce

½ tsp. garlic salt
1 tsp. oregano (optional)
2 loaves small party rye bread

Brown sausage and drain. Brown ground beef and drain. Combine sausage, round beef, cheese, Worcestershire, garlic salt and oregano. Heat over low flame

Lessons Learned on Bull Run Road

until cheese melts. Spread a tablespoon of meat mixture on each slice of bread. Bake at 350` for 10 minutes or until brown. These freeze best if you don't brown them first.

CYNDIE RUSHING GUENARD'S SAUSAGE BALLS

1 lb. sausage
2 c. Bisquick

8 oz. grated sharp cheddar cheese

Mix and roll into small balls. Bake on a greased cookie sheet at 400` until brown.

CHERYL WINSTEAD'S CRAB DIP

1 stick butter
1 bunch green onions
2 Tbsp. flour
1 pkg. Swiss cheese

1 pt. half and half
1 lb. crabmeat
red pepper

Melt butter, add onions and sauté. Add flour and stir. Add half-and-half and Swiss cheese. Heat until hot and melted. Add remaining ingredients.

Shellie Rushing Tomlinson

SOUPS, SALADS AND SAUCES

LETHA DUKE'S SKILLET GUMBO

2 c. diced ham or canned lunch meat	1 (16 oz.) can tomatoes
1 c. chopped green pepper and onions	1 c. chicken broth
1 (10 oz) pkg. okra	1 tsp. salt
	1/8 tsp. Red pepper
	1 c. uncooked rice

Combine all ingredients except rice in heavy skillet. Bring to a boil; cover and simmer for 10 minutes. Stir in rice, replace lid and simmer 20 minutes or until tender.

MARCELLA KING'S CHICKEN AND SAUSAGE GUMBO

1 hen, boiled and deboned	1 bunch green onions, chopped
½ c. oil	1 ½ lb. Smoked sausage
1 large onion, chopped	salt and pepper
1 bell pepper, chopped	file` (optional)

Lessons Learned on Bull Run Road

Roux: Pour oil into thick iron pot over medium heat. When hot, stir in flour and continue to stir until mixture turns a deep brown color. (Usually takes 30 to 45 minutes.)

Gumbo: Brown sausage in different pot and drain. Sauté onions and bell pepper in roux; add one quart cold water to roux. Combine sausage, chicken and broth and add to roux. Add salt and pepper to taste and cook for 30 minutes. Add green onions and cook for 15 additional minutes. Serve over hot rice and sprinkle with file`.

GENEVA ODOM'S FOUR BEAN SOUP

2 lb. Hamburger meat
1 medium onion, chopped
1 whole bell pepper, chopped
1 can pinto beans
1 can navy beans

1 can Great Northern beans
1 can red kidney beans
1 can To-Tel tomatoes
1 can whole tomatoes
salt and pepper

Cook meat, onion, and bell pepper until done and drain grease. Pour beans and both tomatoes in meat mixture. Do not drain juice off beans. Mix all together and let simmer for 30 minutes. Serve with cornbread.

PAPA'S FAVORITE CHILI

4 lb. Hamburger meat
¾ c. shortening
4 or 5 onions, chopped

3 or 4 garlic cloves, crushed
1 Tbsp. black pepper
1 Tbsp. salt

Shellie Rushing Tomlinson

1 can chili powder (small)   red pepper to taste
½ can paprika

Brown hamburger meat with shortening, onions and garlic. Drain off fat.
Add rest of ingredients, then add hot water and simmer for one hour.

JUDY JOHN'S STRAWBERRY MOLDED SALAD

3 (3-oz.) pkg. Strawberry gelatin   1 (20-oz.) can crushed pineapple
   (sugar-free)   in it's own juice
2 c. boiling water   2 to 3 bananas
1/8 tsp. Salt   ½ c. chopped nuts
1 (16-oz.) pkg. Frozen sliced
   strawberries

Dissolve gelatin in boiling water. Slice and stir in frozen strawberries,
pineapple and juice. Place in refrigeration to thicken slightly. Fold in sliced
bananas and nuts. Pour into lightly oiled or sprayed mold or pan. Chill until set.
Spread cream cheese dressing on top or serve separately.

PAM FOSTER'S TOP OF THE RIVER COLE
SLAW

1 head cabbage, shredded   1 medium onion, chopped
1 c. mayonnaise   ½ cup Pet milk
¼ c. sugar   salt and pepper to taste

Lessons Learned on Bull Run Road

Blend all ingredients and pour over cabbage. Toss well just before serving.

RHONDA GOULETTE FOSTER'S LEMON-LIME SALAD

1 (3-oz.) box lemon Jell-O
1 (3 oz.) box lime Jell-O
2 c. boiling water
1 (8oz.) crème cheese

1 can crushed pineapple
1 can condensed milk
1 c. pecans, chopped

Mix Jell-O, water and cream cheese until cream cheese is dissolved. Add remaining ingredients and chill until firm.

MEATS AND MAIN DISHES

HILMA FOSTER'S CHICKEN AND DRESSING

1 hen (5 or 6 lb.)
1 ½ gallon water
4 Tbsp. salt
6 c. corn meal

5 eggs
5 c. milk
½ c. melted cheese
3 tsp. Black pepper

84

Shellie Rushing Tomlinson

3 c. flour	6 boiled eggs, chopped
2 Tbsp. sugar	1 ½ c. bacon grease
2 Tbsp. salt	6 c. chopped onions
3 tsp. baking powder	2 c. chopped celery

Boil chicken slowly until meat drops off bone easily. Debone chicken and save broth for cornbread mixture. Starting with cornmeal, mix next ingredients down to melted cheese. Mix well and bake in greased pans at 400` until done. Crumble cornbread and add pepper and eggs. Sauté onions and celery in bacon grease, being careful not to overcook and lose the flavor. Combine all with cornbread mixture and mix well. Add deboned chicken and chicken broth to mixture. Bake in 350` oven until mixture is brown and "set". This should take approximately 45 minutes. This recipe makes at least three casserole dishes.

CARMEN STONE'S CHICKEN ROLL-UPS

4 chicken breast	½ stick oleo
1 pkg. Crescent rolls	½ cream cheese
1 can cream of chicken soup	½ c. chicken broth

Cook, debone and cut chicken into small pieces (saving ½ cup broth). Put chicken in crescent rolls and roll up. Place in baking dish. Heat other ingredients and pour over rolls. Bake at 350` until rolls are a golden brown.

MAMA'S MEXICAN CHICKEN

1 whole chicken
1 chopped onion
1 tsp. garlic salt
1 tsp. chili powder

½ lb. grated cheddar cheese
1 can Ro-Tel tomatoes
2 cans cream of chicken soup
1 pkg. corn tortilla shells

Boil chicken and remove from bone. Mix chicken, onion, cheese, garlic salt, chili powder and Ro-Tel tomatoes. Butter long casserole dish. Dip tortilla shells in chicken broth and line dish with shells. Spread mixture evenly over shells. Spread cream of chicken soup over mixture. Do not stir! Bake at 350` for thirty minutes or until bubbly.

ARILLA BOUGHTON'S TATOR TOT CASSEROLE

1 lb. ground beef
1 can cream of cheddar cheese soup
1 pkg. Tater Tots

Brown meat and season to taste. Place in casserole bowl. Spread top of meat with cheese soup (better when warm). Layer Tater Tots evenly side by side on top of cheese. Cook until bubbly, 30 or so minutes.

This casserole may be prepared and frozen, and cooked when needed.

Shellie Rushing Tomlinson

SHIRLEY McKASKLE'S SHRIMP ETOUFEE

2 onions, chopped
2 bell peppers, chopped
2 celery ribs, chopped
1 stick oleo
3 lb. Deveined shrimp

1 can cream of mushroom soup
1 can cream of celery soup
1 can cream on onion soup
1 can Ro-Tel tomatoes
½ can tomato paste

Sauté first four ingredients in butter until tender. Add the soups and cook for 15 minutes, then add shrimp. Add salt to taste. Cook 30 minutes and serve over rice.

VEGETABLES

NANA PEGGY'S BAKED BEANS

1 lb. ground meat
1 large onion
¼ bell pepper
1 ½ tsp. Celery salt
½ bottle catsup
2 cans (small) pork and beans

1 Tbsp. chili powder
1 Tbsp. vinegar
salt and pepper to taste
garlic salt to taste
Worcestershire sauce to taste

Lessons Learned on Bull Run Road

Brown meat, drain; add the other ingredients and let simmer for another thirty minutes or longer. Enjoy.

LOU HORATH'S BROCCOLI CASSEROLE

1 c. chopped onions
1 Tbsp. margarine
2 c. cooked rice
1 pkg. chopped broccoli,
    drained and cooked

8-oz. jar Cheese Whiz
1 tsp. dry mustard
1 can mushroom soup
4 chopped boiled eggs
1 can French fried onions

Sauté onions in margarine. Mix remaining ingredients and bake at 350˚ for 15 minutes. Sprinkle French fried onions on top of the casserole. Bake 5 to 10 minutes until brown.

MAMA'S SWEET POTATO CASSEROLE

3 cups mashed potatoes
1 cup sugar
½ tsp. salt
1 tsp. vanilla

½ cup milk
2 eggs, beaten slightly
1/2 stick oleo, melted

Topping:
1/3 c. flour
1 c. brown sugar

1 c. chopped pecans
1/3 stick oleo, melted

Shellie Rushing Tomlinson

Mix first 7 ingredients together and place in buttered casserole dish. Crumble next 4 ingredients and sprinkle on top. Bake at 300` for 35 minutes.

MELISSA TOEWS CORN CASSEROLE

2 cans cream-style corn
1 pkg. Mexican cornbread mix
4 eggs

1 c. oil
4 oz. cheddar cheese of 1
small jar Cheez Whiz

Mix well and bake at 400` for about 30 minutes. Take out of oven and sprinkle with grated cheese.

BREADS, ROLLS AND PASTRIES

RHONDA RUSHING PARKER'S CHOCOLATE ÉCLAIR PIE

1 large pkg. Vanilla instant
  pudding

3 c. cold milk
8 oz. Cool Whip

Topping:

89

Lessons Learned on Bull Run Road

1 c. sugar   ½ stick oleo
1/3 c. cocoa   1 tsp. vanilla
¼ c. evaporated milk

Mix milk and pudding together as directed on package. Stir in Cool Whip. Line bottom of 9x13-inch pan with whole graham crackers. Pour half of the pudding mixture over graham crackers; add another layer of crackers and remaining pudding mix. Top with another layer of graham crackers.

Topping: Mix sugar, cocoa and evaporated milk over medium heat. Bring to a boil, stirring constantly. Remove from heat; add oleo and vanilla. Pour over graham crackers. Refrigerate.

MAMA'S CHOCOLATE PIE

1 ¾ c. sugar   3 c. milk
5 Tbsp. flour   4 egg yolks, beaten
4 Tbsp. cocoa

Stir constantly over direct heat, add ½ stick oleo and cook until thick. Add 4 tablespoons vanilla. Pour into baked pie shell and top with meringue made from 4 egg whites and 6 tablespoons sugar. Bake at 300` until brown. Makes two pies.

JOYCE WILLIAM'S PECAN PIE

½ c. sugar
1 c. white Karo
3 eggs
1 tsp. vanilla

¼ tsp. salt
1 c. pecans, chopped
4 Tbsp. oleo

Mix all ingredients together and pour into unbaked pie shell. Bake 45 minutes at 325`.

MARSHA WILLHITE'S SIX WEEKS MUFFINS

1 (15-oz.) box Raisin Bran
1 c. oil
3 c. sugar
4 eggs, beaten

5 c. flour
1 tsp. soda
2 tsp. salt
1 quart buttermilk

Mix cereal, sugar, flour, salt and soda in a large bowl. Add beaten eggs, oil and buttermilk; mix well. Store in covered container. Keeps up to six weeks in refrigerator. Bake as many as desired at 400` for 15 to 20 minutes.

CAKES, COOKIES AND DESSERTS

CAROLYN GOULETTE'S MILLION DOLLAR POUND CAKE

1 lb. butter, softened
3 c. sugar
6 eggs
4 c. all-purpose flour (plain)

¾ c. milk
1 ½ tsp. Almond extract
1 tsp. vanilla extract

Cream butter, gradually add sugar, beating after each addition at medium speed. Add eggs beating after each one at a time. Add flour to creamed mixture alternately with milk, beginning and ending with flour. Mix just until blended after each addition. Stir in flavorings. Pour batter into a greased and floured 10-inch tube pan. Bake at 300` for 1 hour and 30 minutes or until done. Cool in pan 15 minutes and remove from pan. Freezes well.

MELBOURNE LADIES DUNCAN PLATTERS

2 c. melted margarine
2 c. brown sugar
2 c. white sugar
4 eggs, beaten
2 tsp. Vanilla

2 c. Cornflakes
4 c. all-purpose flour
2 tsp. soda
2 tsp. Baking powder
1 c. pecans, chopped

Shellie Rushing Tomlinson

2 c. oatmeal   1 c. chocolate chips

Mix margarine, sugars, eggs and vanilla. Blend in oats and flakes. Sift dry ingredients and add to margarine mixtures. Add chips and pecans. Chill. Roll in balls; place on cookie sheet about 3 inches apart and bake at 325` for 15 minutes. (You may have to adjust time and temperature to fit your oven.) If baked too long, they are crispy instead of chewy.)

SHELLIE RUSHING TOMLINSON'S HORN TOADS

1 c.Karo syrup   12 oz. peanut butter
1 c. sugar   6 c. Cornflakes

Boil first 2 ingredients; add peanut butter and then Cornflakes. Drop immediately on wax paper. (Work quickly before mixture hardens.)

A TASTE OF BULL RUN ROAD
COOKBOOK INDEX

Lessons Learned on Bull Run Road

VEGETABLES
NANA PEGGY'S BAKED BEANS
LOU HORATH'S BROCCOLI CASSEROLE
MAMA'S SWEET POTATO CASSEROLE
MELISSA TOEWS CORN CASSEROLE

BREADS, ROLLS AND PASTRIES
RHONDA RUSHING PARKER'S CHOCOLATE ÉCLAIR
MAMA'S CHOCOLATE PIE
JOYCE WILLIAM'S PECAN PIE
MARSHA WILHITE'S SIX WEEKS MUFFINS

CAKES, COOKIES AND DESSERTS
CAROLYN GOULETTE'S MILLION DOLLAR POUND CAKE
MELBOURNE LADIES DUNCAN PLATTERS
SHELLIE RUSHING TOMLINSON'S HORN TOADS

Maybe the Bull Run Road Gang has reminded you of days gone by. Every family has their own cherished memories. I hope you'll use these pages I've provided and begin to record yours.

_____

_____

_____

_____

_____

_____

_____

_____

_____

_____

_____

Lessons Learned on Bull Run Road

_____

_____

_____

_____

_____

_____

_____

_____

_____

_____

_____

_____

Shellie Rushing Tomlinson

Lessons Learned on Bull Run Road

_____

_____

_____

_____

_____

_____

_____

_____

_____

_____

_____

_____

_____

Shellie Rushing Tomlinson

Lessons Learned on Bull Run Road

_____

_____

_____

_____

_____

_____

_____

_____

_____

_____

_____

_____

_____

_____

_____

_____

_____

_____

_____

_____

_____

_____

Lessons Learned on Bull Run Road

_____

_____

_____

_____

_____

_____

_____

_____

_____

_____

_____

_____

Lessons Learned on Bull Run Road